What Really Matters in Response to Intervention

Research-Based Designs

Richard L. Allington
University of Tennessee, Knoxville

Boston • New York • San Francisco
Mexico City • Montreal • Toronto • London • Madrid • Munich • Paris
Hong Kong • Singapore • Tokyo • Cape Town • Sydney

Executive Editor: Aurora Martínez Ramos
Series Editorial Assistant: Kara Kikel
Executive Marketing Manager: Krista Clark
Marketing Manager: Danae April
Production Editor: Annette Joseph
Editorial Production Service: Lynda Griffiths
Composition Buyer: Linda Cox
Manufacturing Buyer: Megan Cochran
Electronic Composition: Denise Hoffman
Interior Design: Denise Hoffman
Cover Administrator: Linda Knowles

For Professional Development resources, visit www.allynbaconmerrill.com.

Between the time website information is gathered and then published, it is not unusual for some sites to have closed. Also, the transcription of URLs can result in typographical errors. The publisher would appreciate notification where these errors occur so that they may be corrected in subsequent editions.

ISBN-10: 0-205-62754-4
ISBN-13: 978-0-205-62754-7

Printed in the United States of America

10 9 8 7 6 5 4 3 2   HAM   12 11 10 09

Allyn & Bacon
is an imprint of

www.pearsonhighered.com

Contents

Preface

The *response to intervention (RTI)* initiative has arrived in schools. I would rather it had been dubbed "response to instruction" because improving struggling readers' access to expert, intensive reading instruction is what might make this initiative different from so many that were similarly developed in federal legislation. But I am worried that this RTI initiative may suffer the fate of so many federal legislative initiatives—the development of school programs that help struggling readers but not enough to turn them into achieving readers. That has been the story so far with Title I, special education, bilingual education, and, most recently, Reading First, all initiatives targeted at closing the reading achievement gap between poor, disabled, and second-language learners and their classroom peers.

For me, the reason that these several federal education initiatives have not closed the achievement gap is obvious: Few struggling readers get enough expert, intensive reading instruction to double or triple their rate of reading development. And to actually catch up to their achieving peers, most struggling readers need to double or triple their rate of reading acquisition. Consider the struggling fourth-grader who reads at the second-grade level. If we could design an intervention that would triple his rate of reading growth, from a half year of growth per year to one and one-half years growth per year, it would still require four years of such instruction and growth before he was reading on grade level!

Currently, Title I remedial reading programs add about 2 months' growth per year, and special education programs seem to add no months of reading growth to struggling readers' historical rates of reading growth. But even the 2 months' added growth by Title I program participation is not sufficient for most struggling readers to catch up to their achieving peers. So those Title I students continue to fall further and further behind every year.

The key question is: Why would adding a daily 30-minute remedial reading session be expected to double or triple the rate of reading growth—especially if that 30-minute session is neither added instruction nor expert instruction nor intensive instruction? And yet, 30 minutes of daily intervention instruction is the best most struggling readers can hope for.

In this text I set out an argument for how we might design *response to instruction (RTI)* programs such that struggling readers will develop their reading proficiencies to match those of their achieving peers. In the opening chapters I discuss the problem sketched above in detail. The following chapters are the heart of this book, with each one discussing a factor that my analysis of the research shows is critical to accelerating the development of struggling readers. I close the book with a chapter that offers the questions I have been asked about RTI design and the answers I have given to those questions.

So, I hope this small book helps you design, or redesign, your RTI initiative in ways that result in your struggling readers becoming achieving readers.

Response to instruction efforts that close the achievement gap and turn struggling readers into achieving readers are possible in the schools that we have. This book is intended to provide you with clear and research-based guidance on just how to do that.

Thank you to the followers reviewers for their comments and suggestions: Diana L. Carr, Elgin Junior High School, Green Camp, OH; Barry Hoonan, Bainbridge Island School District, Bainbridge Island, WA; Guyla Ness, Meade School District 46-1, Sturgis, SD; Donna Schweitzer, Forwood Elementary School, Wilmington, DE; and Lisa Wiedmann, former District Director of Reading, Rhinelander Public Schools, Rhinelander, WI.

The What Really Matters *Series*

The past decade or so has seen a dramatic increase in the interest in what the research says about reading instruction. Much of this interest was stimulated by several recent federal education programs: the Reading Excellence Act of 1998, the No Child Left Behind Act of 2001, and the Individuals with Disabilities Education Act of 2004. The commonality shared by each of these federal laws is that each restricts the use of federal funds except for instructional services and support that have been found to be effective through "scientific research."

In this new series we bring you the best research-based instructional advice available. In addition, we have cut through the research jargon and at least some of the messiness and provide plain-language guides for teaching students to read. Our focus is helping you use the research as you plan and deliver reading lessons to your students. Our goal is that your lessons be as effective as we know how, given the research that has been published.

Our aim is that all children become active and engaged readers and that all develop the proficiencies needed to be strong independent readers. For us, strong independent readers are active and comprehending readers. Each of the short books in this series features what we know about one aspect of teaching and learning to read independently with understanding. Each of these pieces is important to this goal but none is more important than the ultimate goal: active, strong, independent readers who read with understanding.

So, enjoy these books and teach them all to read.

chapter 1

Why Struggling Readers Continue to Struggle

Most struggling readers never catch up with their higher-achieving classmates because schools create school days for them where they struggle all day long.

In other words, in most schools struggling readers are lucky if they spend 10 to 20 percent of their school day in lessons designed to meet their needs. Typically those lessons are part of the intervention effort the school has created. But, unfortunately, most of their day, 4 to 5 hours every day, is spent in classrooms where the instruction is targeted to the average achieving student. In other words, struggling readers struggle more because they get far less appropriate instruction every day than the achieving students do.

Think of it this way: That second-grade student still reading at the first-grade reading level often spends his day in a second-grade classroom where almost every lesson is focused on second-grade–level students. (The same situation is usually in place for the ninth-grade student reading at the fifth-grade level—a locker full of ninth-grade–level books he cannot read, but more on this later.) Too often, even the reading lesson is drawn from a second-grade core reading program, a text too hard for that struggling reader. Rarely, if ever, will second-grade students who are struggling readers benefit much from second-grade reading lessons. The lessons are simply over the children's heads, and rarely do the instructional guides provided by the publishers of second-grade reading programs contain useful advice on how to modify, adapt, or replace reading lesson materials so that struggling readers will benefit (McGill-Franzen, Zmach, Solic, & Zeig, 2006).

Reading Lessons, Interventions, and Struggling Readers

Perhaps using grade-level materials to instruct all students is an unintended effect of federal education legislation and the focus these laws have had on creating intervention programs for struggling readers (Title I, special education, English language learners, etc.). The recent No Child Left Behind Act, and especially its Reading First component, has targeted classroom instruction as central to developing a greater number of (basically all) students who read on grade level. These two efforts are among the first federal initiatives to target classroom lessons in addressing the needs of struggling readers. But in many cases these initiatives have been badly misread, and unfortunately, because of the rules and regulations, there are now classrooms that are actually less focused on struggling readers than has been the case in the past. By this I mean that in too many school districts teachers are required, or at least advised, to provide a 90-minute block in some designated grade-level core reading program. In such cases struggling readers will not benefit much from the reading lessons offered.

A Simple but Basic Rule of Learning

Every model for lesson planning begins with selecting print materials appropriate for learners. I have been unable to locate any lesson planning model that suggests that this isn't a critical aspect of effective lesson design. But, on average, most teachers select one text. Most often this text is most appropriate for the average or higher-achieving students. The struggling readers get left behind. One of the key findings of our work studying some of the nation's best first- and fourth-grade teachers was their regular use of what we dubbed the "multi-text, multi-level" curriculum design (Allington & Johnston, 2002; Pressley et al., 2001). In these classrooms teachers selected a variety of texts to teach whatever they were required to teach. They selected some texts that even the struggling readers could read.

Perhaps this is why we were able to document the enormous gains that struggling readers made in these classrooms. These children simply got much more instruction, all day, every day, that both theory and research indicate would allow them to increase their reading proficiencies. A central theme of this book is that struggling readers need a full day, at least, of high-quality lessons if they are to match or even exceed the reading growth patterns observed in their higher-achieving peers.

As outlined in the next chapter, beginning the process of designing school programs that meet the needs of struggling readers has to begin with an examination of the quality of the classroom lessons they are getting. That has to be Step 1 if only because virtually all struggling readers spend the majority of their day in the general education classroom. Thus, it is the quality of the general education instruction that must also match the development of the struggling readers.

Think of it this way: If struggling readers spend their days in classrooms where only grade-level texts (or higher) are used, they are wasting most of their day. It is a waste of time because no theory and no empirical evidence suggest that ignoring the reading needs of struggling readers will produce adequate levels of academic learning. Struggling readers need high-quality lessons *all day long* if they are to ever catch up with their peers.

Different Rates of Learning

There is now good evidence, at least for reading, that almost no students should be lagging behind in their reading development. The federal rules allow schools to exclude 2 to 3 percent of their total student population from meeting adequate yearly progress standards. That means one student in every other classroom will not be required to add at least one year of reading growth, or more, every year he or she is in school. Currently, some 40 percent of students fail to meet this standard. That is almost half of the students!

While mandating virtually all students to the one-year's-growth-per-year reading (and math) standard, the federal legislation assumes that some students are instructionally needier than others. Some students will therefore need more and better reading instruction than other students in order to make the mandated gains. Thus, the federal legislation provides some of the funding that will be necessary to provide that added instruction. These federal funds pay for reading specialists, special education teachers, and teachers for English language learners. These funds also allow schools to provide paraprofessional support.

Perhaps because after 50 years of federal programs where annual gains of one year's growth per year were not expected, much less required, few schools have created classroom or intervention programs that actually produce such growth in struggling readers. The congressionally mandated study (Puma et al., 1997) of the federal Title I program noted that Title I funds have long been spread broadly but thinly. "The level of instructional assistance Title I students generally received was in stark contrast to their levels of educational need" (p. iii). In other words, the federal government never provided sufficient funding to meet the educational needs of all qualified students. Thus, in many school districts the funds were spread about such that some eligible students received some sort of instructional support, but rarely did that support ever reach the level of intensity or expertise that those students needed to achieve a full year's growth, or more, in reading.

> ## Currently special education students don't catch up to peers
>
> Special education placements tend to stabilize reading growth of students with reading disabilities rather than accelerate it. . . . Students who enter special education with reading levels that are two or more years below those of their age mates can be expected to maintain that disparity, or fall further behind. (Denton, Vaughn, & Fletcher, 2003, p. 203)

The results were that, on average, Title I participants added a month or two of growth but never enough to make the goal of adding one year's reading growth per year. Thus, these students fell further and further behind even when they participated in a federally funded intervention. A similar situation describes both special education and English language learner programs. Additionally, little in the earlier federal laws focused on the quality of classroom lessons. Thus, there were too few classrooms where these students had their reading needs met.

Federal law does not ignore the fact that some students find school easier than others. What the law does require, however, is that schools create learning environments where students who need more and better reading instruction actually get more and better reading instruction (Allington, 2006c). What has changed is that federal law now requires schools to show that they are providing instruction that helps struggling readers catch up. This is the "adequate yearly progress" requirement, and it basically requires that schools demonstrate that all students are growing at the rate of at least one year of growth for every year of schooling.

If there is a problem with the federal law, it is that the federal government has not provided sufficient funding to support the programs that will be needed to produce such growth. Personally, I believe that the incentive funding that is provided should be looked upon as a gift to help get schools started down the path of powerful classrooms and even more powerful intervention designs. The problem, then, is that in the end it is the local taxpayers who will most likely foot the bill for more effective schools. In far too many school districts the historical pattern has been to accept the federal money and develop some sort of intervention with that funding. However, the federal funding has never been sufficient to cover the total costs of the sort of high-quality interventions that research indicates could accelerate reading growth. Today, though, too few school boards and central administrations are providing the additional funds needed.

The focus of the new federal legislation is primarily early elementary education, K–3. That is where most of the federal money is targeted. Again, this seems appropriate because the reading gap grows larger every year that struggling readers attend school. The first-grader who is half a year behind his on-level classmates needs far less extensive intervention than the fourth-grader who is two years behind or the ninth-grader who is four years behind. Younger students can catch up faster, or with less extensive and less expensive efforts, than is the case for older readers.

Some students, though, will need extra instructional support even after they have caught up with their peers—not every one of them, but some of them. Using the available data, it is reasonable to expect that almost all of the students who initially struggle can be caught up by third grade. And of those, about half of the students served will remain on level with no added services. However, half will need some instructional support later in their school careers, and a few will need added support all of their school careers if educators expect them to remain on level. Reading development must be monitored so that those students who will need extra support will be located and the support can be provided.

The Essence of the Problem

Some students find learning to read easier than others. For years we have focused mostly on what was "wrong" with those students, and for years we have used whatever we found out to explain why children were not adequately developing reading skills. We often jumped in and provided some sort of support, but too rarely did we believe that whatever we provided was going to help those struggling readers to catch up to their achieving classmates.

So, currently you can walk into almost any fourth-grade classroom and find one or more students reading at the second-grade level. These are students who have been increasing their reading skills at the rate of one-half year per year of school, regardless of what the school has done.

In most cases these students were recognized early, often on entry to kindergarten. The most typical scenario has been that these students were given the "gift of time." In other words, we waited for them to develop. When they didn't, we referred them for more testing and typically for placement in an intervention program (Title I, special education, English language learners, etc.). Sometimes we simply held them back to repeat a grade level in the hopes they would catch up. Yet most never caught up, whether they were provided an intervention or retained in grade. They became the bottom group of students who forever lagged behind their on-level peers.

Doubling or Tripling Reading Growth

Struggling readers have rarely caught up to their achieving peers because most schools have not thought about what sort of efforts might be required to double or triple the struggling readers' learning rates for reading. If a 90-minute reading block is producing a half year of growth, then why would 30 additional minutes every day of large group intervention double or triple that rate of learning? That is assuming that the 30 added minutes are actually added. In most cases, however, that intervention 30 minutes was scheduled during the 90-minute classroom reading block. So no new minutes of reading instruction were added. Instead, we altered part of the 90 minutes of reading instruction but did not add more minutes of reading instruction.

What is worse, perhaps, is that many of those 30 minutes were taught by a paraprofessional. I say worse because there are few people less expert at teaching reading in the school than the paraprofessionals. A large body of research indicates that paraprofessionals do little that actually improves a student's reading achievement in classrooms or either remedial or special education programs (Gerber, Finn, Achilles, & Boyd-Zaharias, 2001; Gray,

McCoy, Dunbar, Dunn, Mitchell, & Ferguson, 2007; Rowan & Guthrie, 1989). These findings are the reason that federal rules on using paraprofessionals have become more explicit and more rigid.

Remember that what I have just described is, in many schools, the best that is available. There are still far too many students who experience difficulty with reading who get no support at all. These students may be retained in grade, but they get no special services to help them develop their reading skills. It isn't because we have no idea of how to create intervention efforts that help all students achieve on-level reading development. A number of such studies are already available (Hiebert, Colt, Catto, & Gury, 1992; Mathes, Denton, Fletcher, Anthony, Francis, & Schatschneider, 2005; Pinnell, Lyons, Deford, Bryk, & Seltzer, 1994; Vellutino, Sipay, Small, Pratt, Chen, & Denckla, 1996). In each of these studies 97 percent or more of all students were reading in the average achievement range after the intervention effort. In these studies rate of reading acquisition was doubled or tripled for participating students. In other words, the interventions were designed to catch up these struggling readers with their achieving peers. These research studies suggest that we have a pretty good idea of how to accelerate the reading development of the instructionally needy students in our schools. The problem: Most schools provide nothing like the interventions that were offered in these studies.

I will also note that each of these studies focused on struggling readers in the primary grades. Studies of techniques used with older struggling readers, grade 4 and upward, have typically shown less success in bringing struggling readers' achievement up to grade level, but that may be a result of the size of the gap in reading achievement these older readers experience. In the early grades it is rare that a struggling reader is more than a year behind. But by fourth grade, one- or two-year lags are common. By sixth or ninth grade, three- and four-year lags in reading achievement are far too common. In these cases it will usually require several years to catch up these struggling readers even if we can triple their reading acquisition rate. There are few intervention studies that last for four years in middle or high school, so there is far less research evidence on just what to do with older struggling readers. Having said that, I will note that doing little or nothing, as is currently the case in too many districts, is a good strategy for fostering dropping-out-of-school behavior.

Building a Reader

When students begin kindergarten, there are huge differences in their literacy development. Some kids have been read over 1,000 books and others but a handful. Some children arrive from preschool programs, and others arrive from home. Some have extensive vocabularies, and others have a far smaller vocabulary. All of this produces some children more ready to read than others. The evidence, however, shows that we can create kindergarten classrooms that reduce, or expand, these initial differences.

McGill-Franzen (2006; McGill-Franzen, Allington, Yokoi, & Brooks, 1999) has developed and tested a kindergarten design that reduces these differences. In this case there are no special intervention teachers. Rather, the kindergarten teachers are provided professional development that fosters an improvement of their classroom early literacy lessons, including daily very small group lessons focused on accelerating the literacy and language development of the children who arrive most at risk of reading failure. Here, the kindergarten teacher simply selects the two or three lowest-achieving children for a daily very small group targeted lesson. The lesson design provides the more expert, intensive, and explicit instruction the lowest-achieving students need if schools expect them to begin to catch up to their more advantaged peers.

It is problematic that few schools consider kindergarten one of the places where early intervention must occur. Additionally, McGill-Franzen's (2006) focus on developing kindergarten classroom teachers' expertise is literally unique in the field. Her design whereby the kindergarten teacher delivers the intervention is also unique. The outcomes of this project have been outstanding and deserve a far broader audience than they have yet received.

So we begin in kindergarten (or prekindergarten if possible) and work harder and more expertly with those students most in need. This begins closing the achievement gap. In first grade the differences in reading development may still exist. So now we create early intervention lists and begin to offer broad extra instructional support to the students who seem the furthest behind their peers.

Each of these early struggling readers must receive a full period of high-quality literacy instruction in the classroom. In two recent studies (McIntyre, Rightmeyer, Powell, Powers, & Petrosko, 2006; Connor, Morrison, Fishman, Schatschneider, & Underwood, 2007) the researchers report that low-

▶ Alaina loves series books.

readiness, entering first-grade students were largely unable to complete much student-directed work they were assigned independently. The most successful first-grade teachers created classrooms where early in the year the students who had developed fewer literacy-related skills spent as much as 70 percent of their reading instructional time in teacher-guided small group lessons. Students with better early skills development spent only about 30 percent of their instructional time in such groups and the remaining time in student-directed reading. However, gradually decreasing the percentage of teacher-directed instruction for the students who arrived with few skills was the instructional strategy that worked absolutely the best.

But Is This Fair?

I mention these two studies because they reflect an important point we observed in our study of exemplary teachers. That observation had to do with what teachers considered "fair." Some teachers, the less effective ones, thought that *fair* meant distributing instruction equally to all students regardless of their needs. The exemplary teachers we studied, however, thought *fair* meant working in ways that evened out differences between students. Early in the year the exemplary teachers largely followed the research by offering greater amounts of instructional time with the poorest readers in their rooms. Gradually the teachers reduced the amount of attention as those children developed better reading skills. The poorest readers in the exemplary teachers' classrooms read as well as the average readers in the more typical teachers' classrooms (Pressley, Allington, Wharton-MacDonald, Collins-Block, & Morrow, 2001).

I have to agree with the stance taken by the exemplary teachers we studied. I do this for two reasons. First, the evidence available shows no negative impacts for assigning the best readers more student-directed work (Connor et al., 2007). Second, since Congress has mandated a substantial reduction in the number of students struggling with reading, the new mindset for schools must be focused on this goal. Providing struggling readers with greater amounts of teacher direction, at least early on, produces improved reading outcomes for these students, and thus the congressional mandate is met.

So How Might This Look in a School?

Figure 1.1 presents the normal bell curve that has been used to describe human cognitive abilities. However, I want to use this curve to suggest something else—typical reading achievement when instruction is common for all students. When all kids are given roughly the same amount of reading instruction of roughly the same intensity and quality, we see reading achievement that looks much like the situation in the normal curve. On the right side of the curve are the higher-achieving students; on the left are the lower-achieving students. In the middle is the middle group of average-achieving students. Most students are in the middle, on or close to grade level.

What Congress has mandated is that federal funding will be used in ways that alter this pattern such that the curve looks more like the one in Figure 1.2. That is, almost all of the students are removed from the far left end of the curve—very low reading achievement has been eliminated.

The only way to create fewer students with limited reading proficiency is to provide those students with more and better reading instruction than that provided to the other students. If we offer all students the same sort and type of reading lessons, we get reading achievement that is spread across the spectrum, as in Figure 1.1. If we offer differential reading lessons such that the students who are behind get more and better reading lessons than other students do, we can achieve a distribution of reading achievement that looks more like Figure 1.2. And schools have been mandated to achieve Figure 1.2.

▶ Figure 1.1 **Normal curve equivalents**

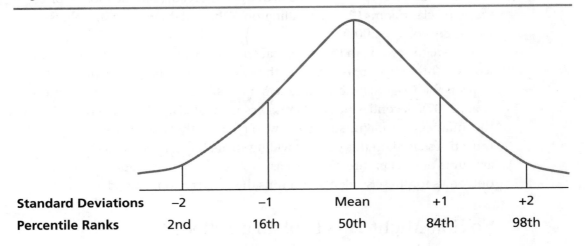

Standard Deviations	−2	−1	Mean	+1	+2
Percentile Ranks	2nd	16th	50th	84th	98th

▶ Figure 1.2 **The bold line shows the expected range of reading scores mandated by Congress under the NCLB Act of 2001**

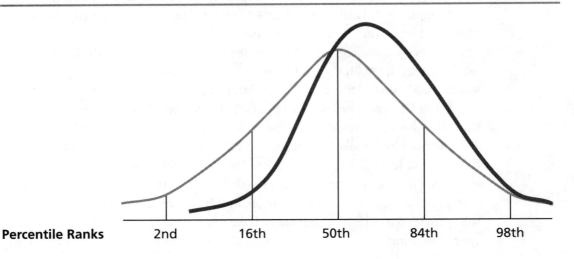

Percentile Ranks	2nd	16th	50th	84th	98th

Given all the bad outcomes in life that are associated with students who continue to struggle to read, I'm reasonably sure that this is a good idea.

Another way of thinking about the typical normal curve is to consider that the further a student's reading development falls below (to the left of) the average reading development of students his or her age, the greater the intensity and expertness of reading instruction that will be required to move his or her reading performance into the average range. All schools have some students who have minimally developed reading proficiencies. But only a few schools have felt charged to provide extra and more intensive and expert reading instruction to the point that those lowest-achieving students achieve reading proficiencies in the average range.

So, in the classrooms we need, struggling readers will get more teacher time, more intensive reading lessons, and, simply, more teacher-directed reading lessons targeted to their specific instructional needs. This will not be easy, nor will it be as hard as it might seem. Taylor's Early Intervention in Reading program (Taylor, Short, Shearer, & Frye, 2007), for instance, created a second daily reading lesson for struggling readers. Similarly, the "after lunch bunch" described by Cunningham and Allington (2007) does the same thing. In both cases higher-achieving students are largely left to read independently while the struggling readers work with the classroom teacher for a second reading period every day.

The success of each of these models has been well described, but neither model actually catches up every struggling reader to grade level. However, both improve the reading levels when compared to classrooms where struggling readers get a single daily reading lesson.

What Does Intervention Beyond the Classroom Look Like?

For the students who are not moving into the average reading achievement range after receiving a second daily classroom reading lesson, schools need to provide something more. The usual name for whatever is provided here is "intervention" or "support services." So what might these "interventions" look like?

Truth be told, I've seen lots of different-looking interventions. At the same time, however, few of these interventions seem well informed by the research we have available. Instead, struggling readers often are sent out of the classroom to work with someone else (or that other person comes into the classroom to work with them). This other person may be a specialist teacher (reading specialist, learning disability teacher, speech and language pathologist, etc.) or a paraprofessional or a volunteer. What we do know is that struggling readers are typically sent out of the room for this intervention during their classroom reading block. Thus, the intervention adds no additional reading lesson time to their school day. Two factors seem important here.

▶ Many struggling readers benefit more from guided reading lessons than from free, voluntary reading, at least initially.

First is the issue of what the struggling reader might miss if he or she is sent out of the classroom at a time other than the reading block time. Second is the issue of ease of scheduling the intervention teacher's time. With the first issue, there is no easy answer but if we intend this intervention effort to close an existing reading achievement gap, then simply replacing part of the classroom reading lesson does not seem a good strategy. Struggling readers need *additional* reading instruction if we expect them to learn to read faster than the achieving students. Replacing part of the classroom reading lesson does not add any more reading lesson time. But if we schedule them out of the room at some other time, they will miss some other instructional segment of the day.

This potential problem may be the best reason for considering after-school intervention designs for many of the struggling readers in your school. Nonetheless, scheduling the intervention reading lessons for times outside the classroom reading lesson time must be done. When to schedule the intervention lesson depends on the reader and his or her classroom. Ideally, it would not be scheduled during core curriculum content classroom lessons, but that leaves little time in most school days to schedule it. We might elect to schedule it during the classroom science, social studies, or health class time, but if so, then the reading materials used in the intervention should be linked to grade-level content in those subject areas. This is not that difficult, but it remains largely unused.

How Much Intervention?

Another problem with most school interventions is that even when they are scheduled outside of the classroom reading block, they typically do not add enough instructional time to be expected to double or triple the student's rate of reading acquisition. Yes, we must double or triple the rate of acquiring reading proficiency. Intervention design must consider that most struggling readers continue to fall further behind each year even when they get whatever intervention is offered (Denton et al., 2003; Puma, Karweit, Price, Ricciuti, Thompson, & Vaden-Kiernan, 1997).

A big part of this problem is that many intervention designs used in schools add a little bit of reading instruction but not enough to double or triple the rate of learning to read. I commonly see intervention efforts that add an additional 90 minutes of reading lessons each week, and those interventions add a month or two of added reading growth. But they do not double or triple the rate of reading acquisition. These interventions rarely help the struggling readers catch up. There is just not enough added reading instruction to accomplish that goal. Thus, we should not be surprised that struggling readers continue to fall further and further behind each year with the small doses of intervention provided.

When we add 90 minutes of weekly small group intervention, about the best we can hope for is a 20 percent increase in reading acquisition or one or two months of added reading growth. For students who are just two months behind their achieving peers that would be sufficient to catch them up. At the same time, most students who are two months behind would not qualify for intervention programs. However, when intervention efforts dramatically increase the amount of reading instruction offered, we are far more likely to see the growth needed to catch up. In one study done by Torgeson and colleagues (2001), they added two daily 50-minute periods of very small group expert intervention for struggling readers in grades 2 through 4 and found that the reading skills gap was basically closed in an eight-week intervention period. In that eight weeks, however, the typical struggling reader received nearly 70 hours of added reading lessons. The typical school intervention effort of 90 minutes each week would have added a little over 10 hours of intervention lessons in the same time period.

If we want struggling readers to catch up to their achieving peers, we must schedule intervention periods so dramatic that increases in reading instruction actually occur. Whether two 50-minute daily reading lessons in addition to a high-quality 90-minute classroom reading lesson are needed is open to question. It does seem, however, that adding about 15 minutes of reading lessons each day is simply insufficient to achieve the on-level reading achievement goal. The same seems true for a daily 30-minute period with older struggling readers.

So how much time does a school community need to schedule for intervention? The simple answer is "enough" to close the reading achievement gap. I note this because if we intend to catch up struggling readers, we will need to schedule sufficient time each day to do so. My guess is that in kindergarten and first grade, most struggling readers will benefit enormously from an additional 30 minutes daily of extra, intensive, and expert reading support. But by second grade and beyond, we will need to schedule more intervention reading time every day. It may be that an extra 30 daily minutes will be insufficient for even some struggling first-grade readers. Although that amount of one-to-one intervention has worked well for those using the Reading Recovery tutorial, it has almost never resulted in every struggling reader achieving on-level reading. Typically between 80 and 85 percent of the students served by Reading Recovery are brought to grade-level proficiency and brought there in 12 to 20 weeks of that intervention (What Works Clearinghouse, 2007).

But that still leaves 15 to 20 percent of the struggling readers struggling. In some cases, extending the length of Reading Recovery intervention would likely bring them to grade-level reading proficiency. In some cases, even that might not be sufficient.

I would suggest that a daily 30-minute expert tutorial or very small group (two or three students) lesson become the basic time allocation model for any intervention intended to close a reading gap. This represents a one-third increase in reading lessons, and this time allocation has been widely studied. There is a good research base indicating the effectiveness of this time period for younger struggling readers (Mathes et al., 2005; Pinnell, Lyons, Deford, Bryk, & Seltzer, 1994; Torgeson, 2002a; Vellutino et al., 1996).

The Bigger Reading Problems

Beyond first grade, longer intervention periods are usually necessary. That is because struggling readers have fallen further behind. By fourth grade there are too many struggling readers who are two full years behind their achieving classmates. It will take greater amounts of reading instruction to ever hope that these struggling readers can catch up. These cases require that we provide something that doubles or triples the rate of reading growth.

If you take a fourth-grader reading at the second-grade level and provide two 30-minute intervention reading periods every day, he might catch up in a year or two or three, or even four. I say this because his historical learning

rate for reading has been roughly a half of a year's growth in each year of schooling. This is the growth rate he has exhibited while receiving whatever reading lessons that have been offered. If you want him to catch up to grade level, you will need to triple his acquisition rate over a four-year period, or quadruple his historical rate of learning over a two-year period.

If you add sufficient time to double this fourth-grader's current reading growth rate, he would still be two years behind peers year after year since he began with a two-year deficit. Doubling that growth rate means he is developing reading skills at a rate of one year per year of schooling. So he never catches up—at least his reading proficiency never catches up with his on-level classmates.

So, although bringing struggling readers' word reading skills up to grade level has been accomplished with older struggling readers, the interventions that accomplished this did not bring reading comprehension and fluency up to grade level (Torgeson & Hudson, 2006). Nor did these interventions make up the substantial vocabulary deficits most older readers have. Now think of a ninth-grader reading at the middle fourth-grade reading level— another struggling reader developing at that same half-year per year. What can be done to bring her reading to grade level before she graduates?

I was visiting a school district this week that provides 25 minutes of remediation every other day to high school students who are struggling readers. That works out to about an hour each week of added reading instruction. Although that is more support than many high schools provide their struggling readers, you should be able to understand why this model does not help many struggling readers catch up. There is good evidence that adding an extra period of high-quality reading instruction to the typical high school day can accelerate reading development but not quadruple that rate of learning to read (Showers, Joyce, Scanlon, & Schnaubelt, 1998).

I would expect that by fourth grade, struggling readers would benefit from a full extra hour of intensive and expert reading intervention every day. For many of these students, this would be sufficient for them to catch up over one year. For others, it would not be sufficient, but it would help close the reading achievement gap. We might consider a two- or three-year intervention plan for these struggling readers, but the goal remains: Struggling readers must catch up.

Response to Intervention

Before closing this chapter I must discuss *response to intervention (RTI)*. Another new federal initiative, RTI derives from the recent reauthorization of the Individuals with Disabilities Education Act (IDEA), the law that provides the federal rules for special education. The intent of RTI is to reduce, perhaps by 70 percent, the number of students who are classified as pupils with disabilities (Lyon, Fletcher, Shaywitz, Shaywitz, Torgeson, Wood, Schulte, & Olson, 2001). Underlying the RTI initiative is the research on early intervention that suggests that many struggling early readers can be caught up to grade level and that currently too many of these students are simply classified as pupils with learning disabilities. Too many are classified without ever having participated in any intensive early intervention.

Response to Intervention

The new IDEA legislation basically attempts to assure that schools have achieved the following (Lose, 2007):

- Provide early identification and intervention with students who struggle with learning to read.
- Develop an alternative method of locating students with disabilities.
- Provide effective, intensive, evidence-based early intervention.
- Monitor each student's progress, using data-based documentation.
- Produce accelerated reading growth to meet annual yearly progress (AYP) criteria.
- Create a multitiered problem-solving team.
- Provide high-quality professional development to teachers of lowest-performing students.

The notion that many struggling readers can catch up—or have their reading acquisition rate accelerated—began largely with Marie Clay, the New Zealander who developed the Reading Recovery intervention (Clay, 1985). Clay advocated providing intensive, expert tutoring to the lowest-achieving first-graders in each school. The goal was to tutor them so as to accelerate their reading development such that they were caught up to their normally achieving peers. Although this intervention has had many critics, the What Works Clearinghouse (2007) has made Reading Recovery the only intervention program to receive the highest ranking for evidence of success. (Chapter 10 contains the WWC ratings of 24 intervention programs that had some research behind them and a listing of over 100 programs that no research supports.)

The review of the research by WWC, D'Agostino and Murphy (2004), and Schwartz (2005) demonstrates that Reading Recovery does accelerate reading development. In fact, the evidence supporting Reading Recovery makes the lack of evidence that the WWC was able to locate for other intervention plans an embarrassing situation. (Go to www.whatworks.ed.gov and click on "Beginning reading" study to see their reviews.)

Reading Recovery has grown over the years since its introduction to North America through the Ohio State University, yet it remains a largely untapped resource used in only some schools. This may be because of its intense focus on training teachers to deliver the intervention design and its reluctance to endorse any intervention design outside of one-to-one tutoring. Thus, Reading Recovery is an expensive proposition at first glance. I say this because when one calculates the true cost of other options (e.g., special education services or retention in grade), using the Reading Recovery intervention with struggling first-grade students is actually less expensive and it enjoys a level of success seldom observed in school intervention designs.

Having said that, let me note that Reading Recovery is one good option for intervening with struggling first-graders. However, first grade is the only place you can use it. There is no second- or third- or ninth-grade Reading Recovery program. This may also be another reason it has not been as widely adopted as might have been expected. But the good news is that we know more about how to design effective intervention lessons that accelerate reading development for struggling readers. I use the term *accelerate* purposely because in order to actually solve the problems struggling readers face every day, they must catch up with their achieving classmates, and accelerating their reading development is the only solution.

What is confusing about the RTI initiative is that although it is a general education initiative, funds can be taken from a school district's special education budget to pay, at least in part, for developing and running an RTI program. Thus, in many school systems today the RTI effort is being headed by an administrator from the special education program rather than a general education administrator. In these cases often a special education teacher delivers the RTI instruction as well. But that wasn't the original plan for RTI.

RTI: Electronic resources

http://blog.reading.org/archives/002225.html

www.hel-earlyed.org/ (click on Jan/Feb 2007 issue)

http://nrcld.org/research/rti.shtml

www.nasdse.org

The original basis for the current RTI initiative was set a decade ago when the IDEA was being reauthorized in 1998. During that time the International Reading Association led a drive to include in that law a requirement that all students struggling with reading receive one-to-one tutoring for one year before they were referred for possible classification as a pupil with disabilities. This effort was based on the research then available that indicated that many early struggling readers could catch up when they participated in expert tutoring (e.g., Lyons & Beaver, 1995; Pinnell et al., 1994; Vellutino et al., 1996). However, that aspect of the bill was deleted as an unfunded federal mandate. Response to intervention then reappeared a couple years later as a special education initiative (Lyon et al., 2001).

But as the National Association of State Directors of Special Education (2007) has noted: "RTI is not something that happens in special education. Rather, it is a method for teaching all students that needs to be driven by general education teachers in the general education classrooms" (p. 2). Basically, the new IDEA requires each state to adopt criteria for determining

Specific Learning Disability eligibility that may no longer require districts to use an IQ discrepancy formula and must permit them to use RTI for that purpose. Because it is based in federal rules and regulations for special education programs, it isn't surprising that many see it as another special education initiative, but it is not.

The other reason for the emergence of the RTI model is the IDEA requirement that schools demonstrate that reading difficulties are not the result of a lack of appropriate reading instruction. Basically, the law says:

> A child shall not be determined to be a child with a disability if the determinant factor for that determination is—
>
> (A) lack of appropriate instruction in reading, including the essential components of reading instruction of the Elementary and Secondary Education Act of 1965;
>
> (B) lack of instruction in math; or
>
> (C) limited English proficiency. (pp. 2705–2706)

The IDEA then requires that all students, and especially struggling readers, be provided appropriate classroom and intervention reading instruction. Only after schools have provided such and documented such instruction and the failure of the student to benefit can the process of consideration for special education begin.

The most appropriate grade levels for RTI initiatives might be in first and second grades and in seventh and eighth grades because those are the grades where most pupils with disabilities are actually identified. On the other hand, there is that evidence about kindergarten interventions as well as evidence on intervening with struggling readers in grades 3 through 5. Again, though, recall that the basic intent of RTI is to provide the intensive instruction that struggling readers will need to catch up with their achieving peers before they are referred for special education services. In many respects an RTI initiative might be placed at almost any grade level where students are referred for screening as pupils with disabilities.

The goal of the RTI legislation is to reduce the number of students who are referred for special education services. The hope is that by providing

One Scheme for Thinking about Struggling Readers and Intervention Design

A Three-Tiered Model

Experts say response to intervention should have several levels of intensity, with instruction provided based on students' individual needs. Currently, this three-tiered model is being popularized. However, nothing in the federal law mentions how many tiers an intervention might include.

75 to 80 Percent

Universal classroom interventions

- All students
- Preventive and proactive

10 to 15 Percent

Targeted very small group interventions

- 2 or 3 students at risk
- High efficiency
- Rapid response

5 to 10 Percent

Intensive, individualized tutorial interventions

- Individual students
- Assessment based
- High intensity
- Longer duration

Source: National Association of State Directors of Special Education (2007).

Iowa's Principles for RTI Design

- All students are part of one proactive educational system.

  All students can learn.

  Use all available resources to teach all students.

- Use scientific, research-based instruction.

  Curriculum and instructional approaches must have a high probability of success.

  Use instructional time efficiently and effectively.

- Use instructionally relevant assessments that are reliable and valid.

  Screening: Collect data for the purpose of identifying low- and high-performing students at risk for not having their needs met.

  Diagnostic: Gather information from multiple sources to determine why students are not benefiting from instruction.

  Formative: Collect frequent, ongoing information, including both formal and informal data, to guide instruction.

- Use a problem-solving method to make decisions based on a continuum of student needs.

  Provide strong core classroom curriculum, instruction, and assessment.

  Provide increasing levels of support based on increasing levels of student needs.

- Use data to guide instructional decisions.

  Align curriculum and instruction to assessment data.

  Allocate resources.

  Drive professional-development decisions.

- Use professional development and follow-up modeling and coaching to ensure effective instruction at all levels.

  Provide ongoing training and support to assimilate new knowledge and skills.

  Anticipate and be willing to meet the newly emerging needs based on student performance.

- Leadership is vital.

  Provide strong administrative support to ensure commitment and resources.

  Provide strong teacher support to share in the common goal of improving instruction.

  Allow a leadership team to build internal capacity and sustainability over time.

Source: Adapted from Iowa Department of Education, 2006.

instructionally needy students with intensive reading interventions, they will be able to demonstrate the ability to catch up with their achieving peers. However, if, after providing appropriate intensive and expert reading interventions through a multitiered design, we have not accelerated a student's reading development, then schools might consider a referral to special education as the last step in the RTI process.

The good news is that we know a lot about how to design effective intervention lessons that accelerate reading development. The RTI needs to be designed to achieve this goal. The main accomplishment of any RTI, then, would be resolving the reading difficulties that some readers experience. Accomplishment of that goal will be most likely if RTI initiatives are designed around core research-based design principles.

The Design of This Book

The rest of this book targets key design features for RTI and other reading interventions. I have identified eight research-based principles after reviewing the research on interventions that accelerate reading development—producing more than one year's growth per year—that must be considered in designing effective reading interventions. Each of the next eight chapters focus on one of the eight research-based principles:

1. Begin an intervention plan. (Chapter 2)

2. Match reader and text level. (Chapter 3)

3. Dramatically expand reading activity. (Chapter 4)

4. Use very small groups or tutoring. (Chapter 5)

5. Coordinate intervention with core classroom. (Chapter 6)

6. Deliver intervention by expert teacher. (Chapter 7)

7. Focus instruction on meta-cognition and meaning. (Chapter 8)

8. Use texts that are interesting to students. (Chapter 9)

As you read this book you will see much of the research that supports each principle. I say "much of the research" because there exists an enormous body of research on interventions, and I present the most powerful studies and meta-analyses of the research on intervention design. To help you evaluate current or planned efforts I have developed the rubric in Appendix A for examining the eight principles of reading intervention design. The rubric presents the likelihood that the design you have chosen will solve the problems of the struggling readers in your school. But before using the rubric, read the book. Happy reading.

chapter 2

Beginning an Intervention Plan

Jerome is a struggling fourth-grade reader. His current reading proficiency is more similar to a beginning second-grader than a mid-year fourth-grader. It's not that Jerome cannot read. He can. But he cannot read fourth-grade–level texts.

He cannot read fourth-grade texts accurately. He cannot read the texts fluently. He cannot read the texts with comprehension. Nonetheless, Jerome has a backpack full of fourth-grade–level texts. He has a fourth-grade reading anthology, science book, and social studies book, and a fourth-grade–level novel, *James and The Giant Peach,* that his district expects all fourth-graders to complete.

But Jerome cannot read any of these books. So why would anyone have given Jerome books that he or she must know Jerome cannot read? Why doesn't Jerome have a desk filled with books written at a second-grade level that cover the core curriculum content for fourth grade? It isn't that such texts are not available. It isn't that such texts are substantially more expensive than purchasing hard books that Jerome cannot read.

So why is Jerome's backpack filled with books he cannot read? I will argue it is primarily because school districts have come to think of intervention for struggling readers as something accomplished in a session outside

▶ Good intervention design must include a focus on classroom reading lessons.

© 2008 Jupiterimages Corporation.

the classroom, a session one period long, a session taught by someone other than Jerome's classroom teacher. School districts have adopted this model, I believe, because federal education policy has long supported such designs (Allington, 2006a).

The current situation in many schools is that struggling readers participate in 30 to 60 minutes of appropriate reading intervention instruction and then spend the remaining five hours a day sitting in classrooms with texts they cannot read, cannot learn to read from, cannot learn science or social studies from (Allington, 2002d). If we enter any school and select any struggling reader (a remedial reader, a pupil with a learning disability, an English language learner) to observe in a general education classroom—a student like Jerome—we typically find that the student has a desk (or a backpack, or a locker) filled with books he or she cannot read. In other words, most struggling readers find themselves spending most of the school day in learning environments that no theory or empirical evidence suggests are likely to lead to any substantial learning.

Why Struggling Readers Usually Continue to Struggle Year after Year

If struggling readers are provided with appropriate instruction only 10 percent of the school day (30 minutes of intervention), one doesn't need to hire a consultant to determine why these struggling readers fail to exhibit the accelerated reading growth that is necessary for them to catch up with their better reading peers. One doesn't need to hire a consultant to determine why certain subgroups fail to make adequate yearly progress if a school's intervention design results in students from these subgroups sitting daily in classrooms with books on their desks that they cannot read.

In every case, such as Jerome's, struggling readers have been improving their reading skills at the rate of less than one year per every year of school. This occurs even when these students participate in an intervention. The crux of the problem for schools is that Congress has mandated that we figure out how to double or triple their rate of learning to read. That is, the No Child Left Behind Act (NCLB) requires that educators do something that will dramatically enhance the development of reading proficiency for any and all students who are currently reading below grade level. Although I have been a critic of the NCLB law (Allington, 2002a), I must note that this focus on accelerating the development of reading proficiency is both research based and necessary. In other words, most schools have implemented some sort of plan that provides struggling readers with a type of intervention but not with the kind of intervention (or classroom lessons) that is likely to dramatically accelerate reading development. In Jerome's case, and most others, he gets some appropriate reading instruction, but he gets less than half as much as his achieving classmates do because his only appropriate reading instruction comes during the 30-minute daily intervention session. Certainly 30 minutes daily is better than no appropriate reading instruction but still far less than is provided to the on-level and above-level readers in his school. No one should think that the school has designed anything for Jerome that is likely to help him catch up his reading skills. Jerome, like most poor readers will simply continue to fall further and further behind each year, even with the intervention effort.

Time to end one-size-fits-all interventions

None of the intervention programs were equally effective for all of the children studied. There may be individual characteristics of children that predispose them to more or less success with a particular program. Research examining this possibility is underway, but it's already clear that we need to move away from a "one-size-fits-all" mentality and apply continuous assessment approaches that evaluate how well an instructional program is working with particular youngsters. (Lyon et al., 2001, p. 277)

What is worse, in too many schools even the supplemental reading instruction is designed to use classroom curriculum texts—that science book or reading anthology or trade book—that the struggling reader cannot read. In other words, the intervention design is one that expects the reading specialists and special education teachers to use the classroom texts in the supplemental intervention lessons (O'Connor, Bell, Harty, Larkin, Sackor, & Zigmond, 2002). This design calls for kids like Jerome to take their classroom textbooks with them when they travel to the special education resource or remedial reading room. Or the design is based on the premise that the specialist teachers will use these textbooks when working with struggling readers in the general education classroom.

No matter, it seems, that those texts are inevitably too difficult. No matter that effective lesson design always begins with selecting texts that are of an appropriate level of difficulty given the skills and development of the learner. This basic design flaw prevails even though we have compelling research evidence demonstrating that using classroom texts—too hard texts—in interventions produces little or no benefit (Allington, 2006c). In a study by O'Connor and colleagues (2002) we see yet another demonstration that using grade-level classroom texts with the truly struggling readers simply doesn't work. On the other hand, O'Connor and colleagues demonstrated that using *appropriately* difficult texts, books at the students' reading level, produced substantive reading growth. Recently, Mathes and colleagues demonstrated that pairing effective supplementary reading instruction with appropriate classroom lessons produces even better gains (Mathes, Denton, Fletcher, Anthony, Francis, & Schatsneider, 2005). None of these findings should be surprising, however. What should be surprising is finding so many schools that still provide struggling readers with texts that are too hard, day after day, in subject after subject.

As a first and most minimal step, we must ensure that supplementary reading interventions for struggling readers are designed in a manner consistent with the scientific evidence. That means, again at minimum, we would not be expecting special education or remedial reading teachers to use the too difficult general education texts that many struggling readers are provided. Instead, struggling readers must be given texts that are *appropriately* difficult, given their level of reading development. Intervention lessons will incorporate these appropriate texts into the core intervention design.

Whenever possible we might select intervention texts that also link to the grade-level curriculum goals and standards (Gelzheiser, 2005; Mathson, 2006). If the social studies focus in the general education classroom is on

state or provincial history, we can work to select texts on those topics that are written at a level that is appropriate for the struggling readers from that classroom. If the language arts curriculum includes the study of biography as a genre, we can locate biographies of appropriate difficulty for use with the struggling readers. In many respects this should be largely the responsibility of the general education staff, but in too many school districts there seems to be scant recognition of any responsibility for supplying appropriate texts for struggling readers. Thus, it may fall to specialist teachers to locate such texts, hopefully in collaboration with the general education teachers who also teach the struggling readers. The goal is to ensure that struggling readers have texts in their hands, all day long, that they can read—texts they can learn science and social studies content from, texts they can learn to read from, texts that are at an appropriate level of complexity.

An Evidence-Based Intervention Effort Is Not Enough

Thinking that supplemental reading interventions alone are the solution to the problems exhibited by struggling readers must be reconsidered. It isn't that such interventions are unnecessary but that they are simply insufficient. All kids, but the focus here is on a certain group of children, need books they can read—accurately, fluently, and with strong comprehension—in their hands all day long in order to exhibit maximum educational growth.

This means that school districts cannot continue to rely on one-size-fits-all curriculum plans and a daily, single period, supplemental intervention if accelerating academic development of struggling readers is their goal. Districts cannot simply purchase grade-level sets of materials—reading anthologies, science books, social studies books—and hope to achieve the goal of accelerating academic development of students who struggle with schooling. There is nothing "scientific" about a decision that content teachers will be provided with 25 copies of grade-level texts. There is no scientific evidence that putting all students in a single instructional material results in anything other than many students being left behind (Allington, 2002d).

Likewise, districts cannot develop a single intervention design, especially one that relies heavily on a single commercial product and material. There is no reason to expect that any single intervention focus will be appropriate for all students who struggle with reading. Some struggling readers do have underdeveloped decoding proficiencies, for instance, but a greater number can decode accurately yet understand little of what they read (Buly & Valencia, 2002; Pinnell et al., 1995; Leach, Scarborough, & Rescorda, 2003). Some comprehend narrative texts far more easily than informational texts. Some exhibit dramatic limits in the number of word meanings they know. Some seem to be able to locate literal information in a text but cannot summarize that same text or synthesize it with other texts previously read. Struggling readers vary on many dimensions, and schools that simply view intervention as requiring all struggling readers to spend 30 minutes each day working with a single product or material will leave many students behind. As NICHD researcher Donna Scanlon has noted,

> However, there are now packaged programs on the market that do not encourage the kind of individualization and responsiveness that characterizes our instructional approach. . . . Cycling students through programs that are not responsive to their needs has the potential to lead to more children being identified as learning disabled rather than fewer. ("New York State Reading Association," 2007, p. 11)

There is no evidence to suggest that effective teaching does not always involve selecting and using curriculum materials appropriate to the academic development of the student. In studies of the nation's most effective teachers, those teachers routinely created "multi-sourced, multi-level" curriculum plans (Allington & Johnston, 2002; Keene, 2002; Langer, 2001) that provided struggling readers in those classrooms with books they could successfully read. That was one of the reasons that struggling readers thrived in their classrooms. I worry that in too many districts struggling readers will continue to struggle because intervention has not been planned as an all-day-long affair. I worry that too many struggling readers spend their days in classrooms using one-size-fits-all curriculum plans—plans that fail to come even close

▶ These students attend a public middle school in Virginia. They are selecting trade books linked to social studies content from a rolling book bin.

to "fitting" the struggling readers in the classrooms, plans that fail the evidence-based criteria.

The most powerful intervention designs begin by focusing on the match between the student and curriculum material, all day long. The traditional intervention design often allowed the district to adopt a single fourth-grade social studies textbook—a book almost always too difficult for struggling readers to learn social studies from (Chall & Conard, 1991). And with the single text adoption, we almost always see whole-class instruction, which is the least effective method of teaching. However, when districts begin to consider an all-day-long intervention design, we see an emphasis on adopting multilevel texts as the basic curriculum. And then we more often see small group instruction common in daily practice. When districts emphasize intervention all day long, we see an increase in side-by-side teaching as teachers spend more time instructing and monitoring individual students. Using multilevel texts in a multisourced curriculum plan literally requires a move away from whole-class lesson designs.

How classroom instruction is organized is also important. The more effective classrooms have a distribution of whole-class, small group, and side-by-side instruction (Pressley, 2006; Taylor, Pearson, Clark, & Walpole, 2000). The more effective schools simply have more classrooms where whole-class lessons do not dominate. The proportion of the school day allotted to whole-class instruction is a predictor of a school's academic achievement. The more whole-class teaching offered, the lower the academic achievement in that school.

Looking at Your School's Instructional Responses to Struggling Readers

We know a lot about effective instruction for struggling readers. To see how well some of the most basic evidence-based principles have been implemented in your school, I've developed two simple data-gathering tools. The first provides data on whether struggling readers in your school have books in their hands that they can read—books that allow struggling readers to learn science and social studies content and that also foster reading growth. The data you can gather using this tool will provide insight on how well your school is responding to the needs of struggling readers.

The second tool provides a snapshot of how lessons are organized in your school. Basically, this tool allows you to examine the distribution of whole-class, small group, and side-by-side lessons in general education classrooms. The organization of instruction is another important factor in how responsive the general education classroom lessons are to the needs of struggling readers. It seems necessary to examine the nature of classroom instruction along with reorganizing the school's reading intervention program.

These two tools provide some very basic information about the lives of struggling readers in your building or district. By beginning with the quality of classroom instruction, you can begin at the root of the problem. Ignoring the quality of classroom instruction provided to struggling readers omits most of their school day from any plan to help these kids catch up with their peers. Omitting 5 of the 6 hours a day that struggling readers spend in school is a bad plan. Next, both of the data-gathering tools are described and their use detailed.

Reader/text matching

To gather classroom information, you will need:

- A notebook folder with a pad of paper
- A ruler
- A couple of #2 pencils
- A pad of sticky notes
- A small calculator
- A timer that can be set to signal when 1 minute has expired

Reader/Text Matching Tool

Begin by gathering the materials listed in the Reader/Text Matching list. Now create a list of all of the struggling readers who attend your school. This list would include those pupils with disabilities and English language learners who exhibit reading difficulties, as well as any student enrolled in a remedial reading program. Once you have the list of struggling readers created, select a 10 percent random sample from the struggling readers attending your school. The easiest method is simply to print out a list of the struggling readers and then select every tenth student on that list.

Figure 2.1 provides an example from a small-town elementary school with 54 struggling readers. I created the tally worksheet simply by drawing 5 columns of roughly equal width for recording data for each student. The goal is a representative sample of struggling readers. The 5 students at James

Elementary School were selected from the 54 students who were receiving Title I remedial reading and resource room special education services.

Once the five students had been selected, I met with each student and spent 15 to 20 minutes with each, collecting words correct per minute (wcpm), accuracy, and fluency data using instructional texts found in each student's desk. I selected four texts for each student (e.g., a core reading anthology, a science book, a social studies book, and so on).

Following the general guidelines for collecting wcpm data, I then had each student read aloud for one minute from each text. I selected where they began to read and marked that spot with a light slash mark. At the end of the minute I placed a slash mark at that point where the student was when the one-minute timer sounded. Later, I counted the total words read during

▶ Figure 2.1 **Reader-text inventory for struggling readers at James Elementary School**

School: **James Elementary**   Date: **January 8**

Student	WCPM		Accuracy		Fluency		Appropriate Books %
Malik 2	31	40	88	91	P	P	0
	39	44	92	94	P	f	
Simone 3	48	49	92	92	P	P	0
	51	43	93	87	P	P	
Rodney 3	61	44	94	89	f	P	0
	52	51	91	92	P	P	
Darrell 4	63	71	88	93	P	P	0
	80	77	94	92	f	f	
RaShonda 5	69	73	90	92	P	P	0
	81	76	93	92	f	f	

the one-minute period and then subtracted all the words that were mispronounced (creating the wcpm data).

While the student read aloud, I kept track of the number of misreadings on my fingers. What you need to keep track of is how many words are misread or simply skipped. When the reading was finished, I put that number on a sticky note and stuck it on the page the student read. I also indicated the fluency rating on the sticky note.

Fluency ratings follow a simple scheme: *Good* means the student read in phrases with expression. *Fair* means the student read in phrases but without much expression. *Poor* means the student typically read word-by-word with little phrasing or expression.

I used the total number of words read in each book and the errors recorded for each text to calculate the wcpm and accuracy data (Mercer & Mercer, 2001) and entered them, along with the fluency rating, on the worksheet (see James Elementary School example).

After the data for each student were gathered, calculated, and entered onto the sheet, I could complete the final column on the worksheet. The key question this procedure tries to answer is: How many of the struggling readers have classroom texts appropriate to their level of reading development?

On the James Elementary School worksheet I derived the percentage data in the final column by looking at how many books could be read at an appropriate wcpm, the average rate for a typical reader at each grade level (Hiebert & Fisher, 2006), and with a 99 percent accuracy and with Fair to Good fluency. This is the traditional independent level—the level of difficulty where students can typically be expected to read a text and understand, or learn, its content with little teacher support (Walker, 2004). This accuracy level may seem high, but consider that a typical fourth-grade novel, say historical fiction, will have between 250 and 300 running words on each page. A 2 percent error rate (98 percent accuracy) means that 5 or 6 words will be misread or unreadable on every page! In a 20-page chapter, the student would encounter 100 to 120 words he or she cannot read. And fourth-grade school textbooks have twice as many words per page, creating the possibility that a reader reading at 98 percent accuracy would be unable to correctly read 10 to 12 words per page, or 200+ words per chapter. That is a lot of words to miss even if accuracy seems high. Using the 99 percent accuracy standard reduces the number of errors above by half—a much more manageable number.

As illustrated in Figure 2.1, struggling readers at James Elementary School are in trouble. None of the struggling students has even a single book that would be considered an appropriate level of complexity. In other words, 100 percent of the texts these students were given are simply too hard for them to learn to read or for them to learn content. Few of these struggling readers are likely to exhibit accelerated reading development, regardless of the nature of the supplemental reading intervention programs they participate in. Most of them are unlikely to acquire much science or social studies knowledge—unlikely because these struggling readers have books in their hands that they cannot learn to read from and that they cannot learn social studies or science or literature from.

Every school should conduct such an assessment of the match between reading levels and the texts students have in their desks. You will need a good idea of the quality of daily instruction each and every struggling reader receives and looking at the reader-text match is a fairly easy way to do that. The question of who will gather such data in your school is up to you. Perhaps a school administrator could do the data collection or one of the specialist teachers.

Here I focused simply on a small group of struggling readers. I selected a 10 percent random sample of the struggling readers because I was interested in developing a data gathering procedure that could be completed in a single morning. You may have a substantially larger number of struggling readers in your building or want to evaluate the matches for a larger percentage of struggling readers. Just remember that you do not usually need to know the reader-text match for every struggling reader. Instead, the goal is to gather sufficient data to draw some firm conclusions about the nature of the classroom lessons these kids are participating in, all day long.

Classroom Lessons Organization Tool

Next, you might gather data on general education classroom lesson organization and delivery. To do this I prepared a second data sheet (see Figure 2.2) using some of the same materials used to create the reader/text matching tool. This sheet has five columns. The first column is a listing of each of the general education classrooms at James Elementary School. The second column is where you mark when you observe a whole class lesson; the third

► Figure 2.2   **Instructional groupings at James Elementary School during the week of January 5 through 9**

School: **James Elementary**   Date: **January 5 - 9**

Classroom	Whole Class	Small Group	Side-by-Side	%
Ka	X X X X X	X X X X	X	50
Kb	X	X X X X X	X X X X	10
1a	X X X X X X X X X X			100
1b	X X	X X X X X	X X X	20
2a	X X X	X X X X X	X X	30
2b	X	X X X X	X X X X X	10
3a	X X X X X X X X	X X		80
3b	X X	X X X X X	X X X	20
4a	X X X X X X X	X X X		70
4b	X	X X	X X X X X X X	10
5a	X X X X X X X X	X X		80
5b	X X X X X X X	X X X		70

column is where you note observing a small group lesson. The fourth column is where you indicate having observed side-by-side teaching (this is when the teacher is working with an individual student). The final column lists the percentage of observations that whole-class lessons were observed.

The data displays in Figure 2.2 were developed from twice-daily quick classroom observations done over the period of one week. In other words, I asked the principal to walk through the building twice each day (varying the time of day the walk-throughs occurred). On each walk-through, she simply entered each classroom and observed the lesson delivery. Then she placed the tally mark in the appropriate column (WC = whole class, SG = small group, S×S = side-by-side). At the end of the week it was obvious that too many teachers delivered too many lessons in whole-group formats.

In other words, little balance in lesson organization was observed in many classrooms, but other classroom teachers did vary the instructional delivery. Research indicates that all students, but especially struggling readers, benefit greatly from this balanced instructional delivery approach (Allington & Johnston, 2002; Pressley, 2006; Taylor et al., 2000).

The Case of James Elementary School

It would be tough to be a struggling reader at James Elementary School, regardless of how effectively designed the intervention programs might be. It would be tough because the best most struggling readers can hope for is one short period daily of effective instruction offered in the intervention programs (and five longer periods where too-hard texts will limit the possibility of learning content or learning to read). Given the focus on whole-class lessons, where everyone is provided the same grade-level text, struggling readers at James Elementary spend most of their school day (4 to 5 hours) sitting in instructional environments that no theory nor any empirical evidence suggests will advance their academic development.

Unfortunately, no intervention product or package will have much impact on the outcomes for the struggling readers at James Elementary School. This school will continue to fail to meet the federal adequate yearly progress (AYP) goals for their economically disadvantaged students and their pupils with disabilities. In too many schools like James Elementary, there will be a gnashing of teeth and strident complaining that it is not fair to expect all students to achieve. No one at James Elementary School or at schools like James Elementary seems to have a clue as to why struggling readers struggle so at their school. No one.

The staff at James Elementary wonder why struggling readers who are lucky to be participating a daily, very small group, personalized reading intervention sessions still never seem to catch up with their achieving peers. No one seems to notice that it is only during that single period each day that the struggling readers are provided with texts and lessons that theory and research support. The other 5 hours each day are largely comprised of texts and lessons that are over their heads. The other 5 hours each day offer lessons that work best for the highest achieving students and don't work at all to help those students who struggle.

No one should expect struggling readers to double or triple their rate of reading acquisition if educators create schools where these children spend most of their time in classrooms where the texts are too hard for them to read. Struggling readers need a full day of powerful and appropriate instructional activities. Before designing your intervention effort, evaluate how many struggling readers will be struggling all day long because they have texts in their hands they cannot read.

Summary

There has been much concern for a focus on "scientific" reading instruction as the best path to ameliorating the inequities in reading achievement typically observed in schools. I support that focus. But little of the guidance provided thus far has focused on the critical factors of reader/text matches and the organizational delivery of classroom instruction. We have had evidence for some 60 years about the importance of these aspects of instructional design (Betts, 1946). Yet, as I walk through schools, even those with substantial federal funding, I too often see classrooms stocked with textbooks that are simply inappropriately difficult for some, if not many, of the students. I too commonly observe a steady reliance on whole-class lessons using these one-size-fits-all curriculum materials. I walk through schools where the only appropriate reading instruction struggling readers receive is that single period each day of supplemental reading instruction. And in these schools no one seems to have noticed that most struggling readers spend most of their school day in instructional environments where no theory would predict they would learn very much.

This is not rocket science. We need to reconceptualize interventions for struggling readers as something that must occur all day long. Intervention cannot just consist of a few minutes working with a specialist teacher. All students need texts of an appropriate level of complexity all day long to thrive in school. In too many schools the texts in students' hands are appropriate for the highest-achieving half of the students. In too many schools we have a curriculum plan that ensures the rich get richer because it is only the best readers who have books in their hands that they can read accurately, fluently, and with understanding. Only the better readers can learn from these books.

When we redesign schools so all students have backpacks (or lockers) full of books they can read accurately, fluently, and with comprehension, we will have schools where fewer students struggle. Only when students have books they can read in their hands all day long can we expect supplemental interventions to make any difference.

Once we have a more differentiated set of curriculum materials, then we might expect a better balance of whole-class, small group, and side-by-side lessons. All students benefit from small group and side-by-side teaching, but it is the struggling readers who seem to benefit most. Perhaps it is because it is these students who have the greatest need for explicit teaching and scaffolded instructional support. It is the struggling learners who are the most instructionally needy and thus benefit the most from the more personalized instruction.

Recent federal legislation has placed a new accountability pressure on U.S. schools to demonstrate that instruction benefits all students relatively equally. Most schools currently work better for higher-achieving students than for lower-achieving students. In other words, some students grow more academically each year and others grow less. In most schools struggling readers fall further behind each year. These schools work better for the higher-achieving students because the curriculum materials and instructional plans are best suited to the needs of those students. Unless that trend ends, many schools will face federal sanctions for failing to create schools that work well for every student.

For too long we have focused our attention primarily on the nature and effects of supplementary intervention programs as one way to address the needs of struggling readers. For too long we have labeled struggling readers and focused on their weaknesses as the root of the problem. Until we recognize that appropriate instruction has to be available to struggling readers all day long, it is unlikely we will meet the challenges of the new legislation and the moral obligation to end the struggles of our struggling readers. Until schools are organized in ways that ameliorate the struggles student face, rather than create those struggles for them, too many students will be left behind.

chapter 3

Matching Reader and Text Level

Whenever we design an intervention for struggling readers, the single-most critical factor that will determine the success of the effort is matching struggling readers with texts they can actually read with a high level of accuracy, fluency, and comprehension.

In this chapter I discuss what research says about what levels of text reading accuracy are optimal and options for finding those texts for the struggling readers you will be working with.

Research on Accuracy Levels and Accelerated Reading Growth

Let me begin by noting that very few intervention studies have actually documented the accuracy levels of struggling readers. I am unsure why this is, but the good news is that the available research is quite consistent: High levels of reading accuracy produce the best reading growth. Consider the recent study of the accelerated reading outcomes in a tutoring program in New York City: "The reading achievement of students who received tutoring appeared to be explained primarily by one aspect of their tutoring experience—reading texts at a high level of accuracy, between 98% and 100%" (Ehri, Dreyer, Flugman, & Gross, 2007, p. 441). In other words, when the struggling readers read routinely from texts that they could read at the historical "independent" reading level (98 to 99 percent accuracy), they made the greatest reading gains. This is a critical finding. This is also a finding that has other support, but that support seems to have been largely ignored.

Historically, we can turn to the early work of Emmett Betts (1946) who, more than a half-century ago, studied and then developed guidelines for three levels of text difficulty. He argued that the *independent* reading level was found in texts where the student could read with complete understanding and freedom from frustration. The *instructional*-level text was the text where the student could read satisfactorily with teacher direction and guidance. His *frustration*-level text was one where the student struggled with words, ideas, and fluency. Betts argued that frustration-level texts should be avoided. He also set guidelines for oral reading accuracy for each level.

> *Independent level*: "At the primary-grade level, no more than one 'new' word in 200 running words should require study; at the intermediate-grade level, no more than one 'new' word in 100 running words" (p. 274).

Instructional level: "For the instructional reading level, a child should meet a maximum of one 'new' word in 20 running words. A better average for many pupils is in the neighborhood of one 'new' word in 50 or 60 running words" (p. 274).

Using these guidelines, we can establish accuracy standards using percentage of words correctly read, assuming the "new" words Betts refers to would present the reader with potential word recognition difficulties. For Betts, then, anything less than 99 percent accuracy was considered too difficult to be independent reading (reading not done in a guided reading group). For guided reading lessons, his recommendations are for texts that can be read with between 95 and 98 percent accuracy. Figure 3.1 summarizes Betts's recommended levels of text reading accuracy. I highlight Betts's 50-year-old criteria because I think that, in addition to his early work, most studies that have documented the reading difficulty of texts support his findings. In addition, my own clinical experiences support his standards.

Other researchers have found that what I have called "high-success reading" activities produces more growth than reading lessons using harder texts (Allington, 2006c). For instance, Fisher and Berliner (1985) studied reading development in a number of classrooms and concluded: "The data indicate that high success during instruction is especially crucial to the learning rate of low achieving students" (p. 224). They found that struggling readers who

▶ Figure 3.1 **Recommended oral reading accuracy levels of text difficulty**

Independent reading, such as content area textbooks, voluntary reading texts, or any text not part of a small group guided reading lesson	99–100%
Instructional reading, such as that done in small, guided reading groups	95–98%
Frustration reading is to be avoided	less than 95%

Source: Betts (1949).

experienced classroom lessons where the reading activities were high-success activities produced far greater gains than classrooms where struggling readers read harder texts. Their findings might have produced significant attention to using high-success texts with struggling readers, but it did not seem to have that effect.

O'Connor and colleagues (2002) found that roughly 80 percent of intermediate grade resource room interventions used grade-level classroom texts in their instruction. That is, a fifth-grade student with reading difficulties brought one of his fifth-grade–level classroom texts (basal reader, science book, social studies book) to the resource room for use in his intervention lesson. O'Connor and colleagues compared tutoring in grade-level texts with tutoring using reading-level texts. The fifth-grade struggling readers who used the grade-level texts benefited little from the tutoring when compared to the gains made by the struggling readers tutored using texts matched to their reading levels. (In this study a fifth-grade struggling reader with a third-grade reading level was tutored in third-grade–level texts in the matched reading-level tutoring treatment.)

Overall, O'Connor and colleagues' (2002) findings indicated support for my high-success reading argument. They concluded their study by noting: "The proposition that poor readers will make stronger comprehension gains by reading in grade level texts with appropriate support (e.g., assisted reading) was not borne out here" (p. 483). In other words, reading third-grade–level texts produced accelerated reading growth for the fifth-grade struggling readers, but reading, or attempting to read, grade-level texts did not. This finding is critical when considered alongside the findings from Ehri and colleagues' (2007) study. In both cases, high-success reading was the critical factor in accelerating reading development both in the study with first-grade struggling readers as well as in the other with third- and fifth-grade struggling readers. In addition, both studies were published in superior-quality research journals, which only adds to their credibility.

Finally, we could examine the findings of a recent large-scale meta-analysis. Swanson and Hoskyn (1998), after reviewing over 900 studies of interventions, also found that matching students' reading abilities with the texts they had to read was one of only three aspects of intervention design that predicted reading growth.

Estimating Difficulty Before Having Students Read

It is always useful to have some idea just how difficult a text might be before you consider assigning it to students to read. Historically, teachers have used traditional readability formulas as the primary tools for estimating text difficulty. The problem is that some of these formulas work far better with beginning reading materials and others work better with materials for older readers (Mesmer, 2008). In addition, there are newer techniques for estimating the difficulty of texts. The quantitative techniques (Lexiles, DRP) are computer-based tools and the qualitative techniques (Reading Recovery, Fountas and Pinnell) use skilled adults to judge the difficulty of texts.

Following is website information for accessing lists of leveled books. For the quantitative tools, I suggest you use the Spache or Fry formulas grade 2 and below and the Dale-Chall or Lexile tools for grade 3 and above.

Spache and Dale-Chall formulas: **www.interventioncentral.org/htmdocs/ tools/okapi/okapi.php**

Fry formula: **http://school.discoveryeducation.com/schrockguide/fry/ fry2.html**

Lexile tool: **www.lexile.com**

Reading Recovery levels: **www.rrcna.org/rrcna/membership/books.asp** (must be a RRCNA member and provide $10.00 payment)

Fountas and Pinnell book levels: **www.fountasandpinnellleveledbooks.com** (requires a $15.00 payment)

Are There Alternatives to Reader/Text Matching?

While the issue of high-success reading activity is critical, Stahl and Heubach (2005) provide an alternative view, at least of the role of more difficult texts in primary-grade classroom reading lessons. They report on a study where classroom teachers, following a district mandate, used grade-level reading materials with all students even though many students read well below grade level. In this case they worked with classroom teachers to adapt the usual reading lessons such that the struggling readers engaged in much rereading of the grade level materials.

In this two-year development project, the features of the reading lessons included use of an oral recitation lesson format with a story map introduction (Rasinski & Hoffman, 2003), with the teacher reading the classroom text story aloud, and with repeated readings of that story that included teacher-led choral readings, partner readings, and home rereading of the story. Kids who needed extra help were given echo reading or had one section of text targeted for fluency. In addition to all of this, students also had 20 minutes each day for self-selected reading activity. Students' reading growth over the study period was greater than expected. Only 42 of 152 students began Year 1 reading on level, whereas all but 11 students ended Year 2 on level. Students made average gains of 1.88 and 1.77 grade levels in Years 1 and 2, but each student read and reread the classroom texts multiple times (15 to 20 times each week).

I have included this study because too many classroom reading lessons are still tied to using the grade-level basal reading series. Those series have few supports to help teachers adapt their lesson design to meet the needs of struggling readers, and rarely do these series have alternative texts that teachers could use that would better meet the needs of the struggling readers. In these cases, the Stahl and Heubach (2005) lesson redesign would go a long way toward providing lessons that would benefit the struggling readers in such classrooms, and classroom reading lessons are an important factor in accelerating reading growth.

I would explain these findings by noting that the appropriate text reading level for a given child is typically inversely related to the level of support given to the reader. In other words, teachers can make harder texts easier for struggling readers in several ways. Stahl and Heubach note just two of those ways—lots of prereading support and lots of practice rereading the texts.

Why High-Success Reading Is Critical

Why is high-success reading activity so critical? First of all, success breeds success. When readers are successful, that success builds all sorts of motivational aspects about reading activity. More reading produces better reading.

Second, all readers, and struggling readers especially, need high-success reading activity in order to consolidate their growing use of complex cognitive skills and strategies.

High-success reading is accurate reading, fluent reading, and reading with understanding. Unfortunately, struggling readers typically engage in very little high-success reading (Allington, 1983, 2006b; Hiebert, 1983). However, when struggling readers do engage in lots of high-success reading, their reading improves, typically dramatically and often in very short periods of time.

Successful adult readers rarely encounter difficult reading (and when they do they often simply stop reading that text). Successful adult readers prefer high-success reading over hard reading. That is one reason most adult reading is in texts with a high school level of difficulty (or lower). Few adults read *Science* magazine compared to the number who read *People* magazine. Far fewer people read *Scientific American* than read *Entertainment Weekly*. Most newspapers and popular magazines are written at a middle school level of difficulty. Think back to your typical daily reading: Do you recall finding words on every page that required a fair amount of attention to decode? Many words that you could not decode?

Think of it this way, a 5 percent error rate (95 percent accuracy) produces a lot of word reading difficulties in typical texts. Table 3.1 illustrates this with texts written for readers at different levels of development. In creating Table 3.1 I simply used several texts from our home library. As you can see, a 5 percent error rate in a popular adult paperback produces almost 20 words on every page that cannot be read easily (or at all). Even reading at a 99 percent accuracy would likely be too hard for most adults to consider. The paperback version of *The Secret Life of Bees* that I used has chapters that run about 30

▶ Table 3.1 **Oral Reading Errors per Page at Different Levels of Accuracy**

	95%	98%	99%
The Secret Life of Bees (Sue Monk Kidd)	18.5	7.4	3.6
My Brother Sam Is Dead (J. & C. Collier)	15	6	3
The Magic School Bus (Joanna Cole)	6	2.4	1.2

pages. At 3.6 "new" words per page, the reader would encounter over 100 such words in every chapter. If those words could not be correctly read or read correctly only after slowing down to decode each one, that book would be a hard book! At 300 pages in length, the reader would encounter over 1,000 such words. And that is if he or she reads with 99 percent accuracy. If we used the 95 percent accuracy standard, the reader would see over 5,500 such words.

But the truth is that people who select *The Secret Life of Bees* to read probably read the book with something more like a 99.999 level of word reading accuracy, which means that they encountered 3 or 4 words that required them to slow down and decode. That is high-success reading.

But even a child reading *The Magic School Bus* series would see a lot of words that will take time to decode (or maybe take the time and remain read incorrectly). At roughly 40 pages in length, a 5 percent error rate produces almost 250 words that cannot be read easily. Even at the 99 percent accuracy level, the reader encounters almost 50 words that will take time to read (if they can be correctly read at all). That's a lot of hard words—and successful adult readers do not seem to like texts much with lots of hard words.

One simple strategy for examining the role of high-success texts in reading development is to gather data on the reading accuracy of readers of different reading achievement levels in your classroom. Unless your classroom is very different from most classrooms, you would find that your best readers have desks full of high-success texts. Your struggling readers, though, are not so lucky. In most schools the best readers read all day in texts that produce high levels of success. The texts the good readers read are read accurately, fluently, and with comprehension. This steady diet of high-success reading is what produces their above-average reading growth, year after year. Imagine what might happen if struggling readers had desks full of high-success texts. Imagine if whatever reading intervention they go to used high-success texts for the intervention reading lessons.

Motivational Gains

High-success reading produces a motivation to read. Guthrie (2004) has noted that reading engagement requires students who are actively using cognitive processes while reading with an emphasis in either cognitive strategies or conceptual knowledge or both. This is purposeful reading, intrinsically motivated, and socially interactive.

Guthrie notes that the correlation between engaged reading and comprehension on the National Assessment of Educational Progress was stronger than any demographic characteristic (socioeconomic status, family background, income, ethnicity, gender). In other words, more highly engaged readers from homes with fewer material or educational advantages routinely outperformed less engaged readers from more advantaged home environments. He argues, "Based on this massive sample, this finding suggests the stunning conclusion that engaged reading can overcome traditional barriers to reading achievement, including gender, parental education, and income" (2004, p. 5).

Engaged reading is motivated reading. Guthrie, Wigfield, Metsala, and Cox (1999) report that reading motivation predicts reading volume (with other factors controlled) and reading motivation directly predicted reading comprehension performance as well. Unfortunately, as students progress through school, motivation for reading declines. This is most obvious in struggling readers who often engage in no voluntary reading after grade 3 or 4 and read only on demand.

By providing struggling readers with easy access to appropriate texts, we may be directly addressing this motivational problem. But no matter how high-success reading affects reading motivation, it also improves achievement.

Learning more about text difficulty

Heidi Anne Mesmer (2008) has written a comprehensive but plain-language book on text difficulty that will be a wonderful resource for teachers more interested in how to estimate text difficulty. In this short book (150 pages) Mesmer reviews traditional readability formulas and gives good advice on which of the various formulas to use for which grade levels and also notes just how the formulas were created and researched. She covers the more qualitative techniques (e.g., Reading Recovery, Fountas and Pinnell, Developmental Reading Assessment, and others) for estimating text difficulty and begins to sort out the confusion. If your school is interested in developing a high level of expertise among teachers on text difficulty, Mesmer's book would be great for a teacher professional reading group to study together.

Cognitive and Conceptual Processes

The second reason high-success reading is critical is the role of cognitive and conceptual processing in engaged reading. In other words, to be actually reading means the reader is using, purposely, various cognitive skills and strategies while reading. If cognitive processes were absent, we would call it word calling, not reading.

A number of critical cognitive processes are involved in engaged and motivated reading. These range from deciding on word recognition strategies to use to deciding whether to:

- Skim or study the text material
- Summarize or critique the text
- Create mental images or take notes, or both
- Slow down or speed up reading

Every skilled reader makes these sorts of decisions every time he or she reads. But to use any of these cognitive strategies, the reader has to have sufficient brain space available. When most brain space, or cognitive capacity, is being used trying to figure out how to pronounce many of the words, then there is simply not enough space left to use the recommended strategies.

Imagine you are a new driver. You are still at that point where you have to think about everything related to driving the car, even little things such as turning on your blinker before turning. So you are driving and have a talkative passenger. Traffic is heavy on the two-lane road, and you are looking for a particular business address. Your passenger is not helping, however. Instead, he is talking to you about the meeting you are driving to, giving details on the contract you will be negotiating, asking your opinion on options that you will have to consider at the meeting. Because driving is not yet a largely automatic activity, you cannot pay attention to the car, the road, the signs, and the passenger. So what do you do?

This situation is a bit like being a struggling reader who is trying to read a too-hard text: facing lots of demands on your attention—too many demands. Do you skip over the word you know you just mispronounced and keep on reading? Or do you slow down and try to decode it again? If you slow down to decode, most of what you've already read, at least in the sentence that word appears in, will be lost from short-term memory. So after you decode the word, you'll have to decide whether to begin again by rereading the sentence or just move on and not understand the text. The same is true even if you cannot decode the word. Now toss a teacher and some other students into the mix. Have them "help" you by saying the word or telling you to "sound it out." At this point, imagine trying to implement a strategy that you know for enhancing comprehension. Perhaps visualization of the setting. Where in the brain do you have space to do this? The correct answer is: Nowhere.

But slowing down and rereading are the two most common repair strategies that good readers use when they encounter difficulty with a text (Walzyck and Griffith-Ross, 2007). It is just that they encounter far fewer difficulties than struggling readers most of the time because they have texts they can actually read accurately.

One reason high-success reading is critical in improving the reading proficiencies of struggling readers is illustrated here. In order to read well, readers need to have texts they can read accurately. That accurate reading leaves brain space available for all the other stuff proficient readers do while they read. A steady diet of too-hard reading produces struggling readers rather than resolving their problems.

The conceptual aspect of engaged reading largely involves comprehension. It makes no sense to a successful reader to read anything that cannot be comprehended. But many struggling readers plow ahead through texts they do not understand. They plow ahead usually because someone assigned that text to be read (and often that someone is sitting right there next to the struggling reader).

Usually even "word reading" is easier if the student understands the text he or she is reading. For instance, consider these two sentences:

- The boys gawked at the tears on her face.
- The boys gawked at the tears in her dress.

Few proficient readers pronounce the sixth word in each sentence the same (they read them as /teers/ and /tares/). If I had created two passages, each with one of the sentences in it, I can assure you that no proficient reader would misread the words. The point is that context supports word recognition. The sentence or even the story context cannot typically tell the reader the correct pronunciation, but it can help. When a child is reading with understanding, then word recognition typically improves. When reading with little or no understanding, even the reader's word recognition will be impaired. Additionally, most good reader strategy use is motivated by comprehending difficulties or comprehension goals. However, severe comprehension difficulties can also suppress strategy use and reduce readers to simple word callers, at best.

A Final Reason for High-Success Reading

In order to be a fluent, comprehending reader, the individual must be able to read most words in a text with little effort or attention. Most words need to be at-a-glance words (Allington, 2009). By "at-a-glance," I mean words that are recognized virtually as soon as the reader sees them—recognized in milliseconds. By "most words," I mean 99 percent or more of the words.

Good readers can read fluently because they can read almost all of the words accurately while using little cognitive attention to pronounce them. The at-a-glance word pool grows slowly at first, which is why reading fluently in first grade is usually accomplished only after several readings of a story. In fact, I think that one reason that beginning readers are so eager to read and reread texts is that they can literally feel themselves become fluent as they reread a text.

As people read, they add new at-a-glance words to their reading vocabularies. The best evidence we have for this is that typically when 10 to 20 successive readings of a word are correct, that word becomes an at-a-glance word. Some words may be learned faster, some may be learned more slowly. But as people read a "new" word, first perhaps slowly, then faster, finally they will recognize the word as soon as they see it. In order to develop this at-a-glance word store, it is necessary to read and necessary to read accurately. By the middle of first grade, pupils have begun the development of this at-a-glance vocabulary. At first it is the frequent, small words that become at-a-glance words, such as *the, is, was, come, go,* and *run*. All of these words are part of the earliest words on the Dolch word list (Dolch, 1936). Way back then, it was clear that just a few frequent words comprise the majority of all the words we read. Dolch identified 220 such words for learning in grades 1 through 3. They have been dubbed the "basic sight vocabulary for reading English" because those 220 words make up more than half of all the words an English reader will ever read. But those 220 words are just among the most frequent words, and by third grade the achieving readers know a few thousand words at a glance.

So how does a third-grader develop, say, a 2,000 at-a-glance word vocabulary? Mostly by just reading (Adams, 1990; Cunningham et al., 2002; Share, 1995). It is the frequent reading, primarily high-success reading, that allows the reader to encounter lots of words many times each. Of course to engage in high-success reading means that this reader also has to be able to decode so that when she encounters a "new" word for the first (and second, third, . . . tenth) time, she reads it correctly. But decoding difficulties, although present in some struggling readers, have not been found to be the most significant factor observed in struggling readers in fourth or ninth grade (Buly & Valencia, 2002; Brasseur & Hock, 2006). In fact, for many struggling readers decoding is a strength, on grade level, whereas comprehension, vocabulary knowledge, fluency, and other factors lag well behind grade level.

Decoding problems stem largely from inexact or insufficient teaching. When beginning readers are given explicit decoding instruction that introduces the basic scheme that underlies any alphabetic language, they become competent decoders. But when such lessons are either minimized or exaggerated, students suffer (Foorman, Francis, Fletcher, & Schatschneider, 1998; Phillips, Norris, & Steffler, 2007). It is good, balanced, reading lessons that produce good, balanced readers. Teach decoding, and teach the other skills and strategies also, and always give students lots of opportunities to engage in high-success reading. That's how you can build real readers from struggling readers.

Stamina

One final topic must be considered when thinking about high-success reading: stamina. By "stamina," I mean the ability to read independently for rather long periods of time. I assume reading stamina is developmental, that readers develop greater and greater stamina for reading as they improve their reading proficiencies and extend their reading practice. For me, stamina is the ability to read a book uninterrupted. As adults, we don't often do this but most of us could if we wanted to, needed to, or just had that big block of uninterrupted time. But many struggling readers, even older struggling readers, seem unable to read for much more than 15 minutes uninterrupted (Samuels & Wu, 2003). I think this is a result of two possible factors.

First, we have not expected struggling readers to read much, ever. Therefore, like a sprinter, who is fast over short distances, finishing a 26-mile marathon race may be problematic. The struggling readers may be, likewise, untrained and unpracticed at reading uninterrupted for longer periods of time. Second, if struggling readers have not yet developed a large store of at-a-glance words, then reading will require more effort than it does for readers with a large at-a-glance word recognition vocabulary. But the only way to build the larger at-a-glance word recognition vocabulary is to experience lots and lots of high-success reading.

So my final thought here is that we must work to increase the amount of high-success reading that struggling readers do. This may involve scheduling several shorter periods each day with the goal of lengthening those periods until adequate reading stamina is developed.

Summary

Providing lots of high-success reading opportunities is one critical component of any research-based intervention design. That means working hard to put these texts in struggling readers' hands (and desks and backpacks). We can create multilevel, multisourced curriculum that help us accomplish this goal. But we must also support classroom teachers in the use of such curricula. Remember, intervention has to be something that happens all day long.

You cannot learn much from a book you cannot read accurately, fluently, and with understanding. We need to ask ourselves whether we have created classrooms and intervention designs where high-success reading is the normal course of events. If it is not, then we must begin our work to address that problem.

chapter 4

Dramatically Expanding Reading Activity

Too often we have designed reading intervention programs where the students engage in everything but actual reading. That is one reason intervention seldom accelerates reading growth.

After reviewing the research on intervention I will suggest that those interventions that are likely to accelerate reading growth—that is, produce more than one year's growth per year—have struggling readers engaged in reading high-success texts for roughly two-thirds of the intervention period. This typically doubles the volume of actual reading that struggling readers do every day. It is this dramatic increase in reading volume that produces the accelerated reading growth. In this chapter I will review the research that led me to this conclusion and offer advice on how to create interventions that provide such massive amounts of additional reading practice.

Why Reading Activity Is Critical in the Development of Reading Proficiency

Reading is like every other human activity in that the amount of practice really matters, especially the amount of reading done while reading proficiency is being developed. The role of *volume* of reading—my term for the amount of reading activity—can be compared to the role of the amount of bike riding children might do.

When younger children are learning about riding a two-wheeler, it takes a fair amount of successful bike riding to begin to develop the basic skills needed. That is one reason many kids learn on bikes with training wheels. It is also why parents end up pushing the child to get them started. But riding a bike with training wheels isn't the goal. However, balancing oneself on a two-wheel bike while pedaling and negotiating a sidewalk or street is absolutely essential, and balancing while pedaling has to be learned. Like reading, no one is born knowing how to pedal and balance simultaneously. Guidance, support, and practice are needed.

After a few days (or weeks) of riding with training wheels, those wheels are removed and the real test arrives—riding a two-wheel bike without the training wheel support. Notice I wrote, "days (or weeks)" of the training wheel supported practice. I wrote it this way because how long to leave the training wheels on is a function of several factors, but the two most important seem to be how many hours of training wheel supported practice the child engaged in and the child's level of confidence that he or she is ready to go it alone without the training wheels. A third factor, as always, is individual differences in children's readiness and interest in learning to ride a bike, but that variation seems less important in most cases than the first two factors.

When a child is excited about learning to ride a bike and when that child has been successful and supported during the training wheel phase, no one should be surprised when the child rides the two-wheel trainer for an hour or more every day. As far as I know, there is no magic number of hours of such bike riding practice that has been documented as the essential minimum. But the more training wheel bike riding practice, the better seems to be the basic rule if moving on to riding a two-wheel bike without training wheels is the goal. However, if the training wheels are poorly installed or the bike seat height is set so that the child cannot fully pedal all the way around or the child is not very interested in riding this new bike that grandpa bought for him, then attempts at practice will be less successful and less common, and we may never get a bike rider.

If everything works well, though, in a few days (or weeks) we will have a child now riding a two-wheel bike without training wheels. At that point, the basic skills have been mastered. The child may be happy with that accomplishment. Some kids, however, want to become more proficient bike riders, perhaps even competing in bike racing or bike stunt events. In such cases it will take many more hours of bike riding to develop the bike riding skills needed. Reading is a lot like that, except that in our society no one is actually asked whether he or she wants to read better. One problem we face as teachers is that standards for reading proficiency have been set by others, and all children are supposed to achieve those standards, whether they want to or not.

A second problem with learning both bike riding and reading arises when the initial attempts are not successful. In both cases, motivation for learning (to ride a bike or to read independently) can be squashed by initial failure. Since we have no federal bike riding standards that all children must achieve, this is less of a problem when failure occurs in learning to ride a bike. But when children fail to learn to read, we cannot simply allow them to choose to be nonreaders. Instead, we must work hard to overcome their resistance and develop their reading proficiencies.

The key point here is that practice is always important in the development of proficiency. Also important is initial learning support and success. The problem teachers face in working with struggling readers is that they are working with students who have not been successful initially, so typically their enthusiasm for learning to read has been reduced, which means that their interest in engaging in reading has also been reduced. In short, they practice reading so little that little reading development occurs.

I must note, though, that it isn't just that struggling readers don't like to read and so they don't but that we have typically organized schools such that struggling readers spend large parts of their days in environments where there are few texts they can actually read. We even create instructional environments, including interventions, that offer very limited opportunities to read. Instead, we have struggling readers working on their reading skills and not working on actual reading (Allington & McGill-Franzen, 1989; McGill-Franzen & Allington, 1990; Rowan & Guthrie, 1989; Vaughn et al., 2003; Ysseldyke, O'Sullivan, Thurlow, & Christenson, 1989). In other words, in study after study of intervention programs, researchers have reported that struggling readers actually read less than 10 minutes of the intervention block, and far too many report that struggling readers never read text during their intervention lesson.

It's the same as if we designed bike riding so that children never actually got the bike, much less the training wheels and the practice. Instead, our bike-riding introduction would have a pedaling machine, not a bike, and a handle bar machine, not a bike, and a bike seat on a balancing bar, not a bike. Our bike riding would consist of the child working on each machine and answering questions that we pose about what we just said, but no bike riding with or without training wheels! I suspect that no one reading this book would create such a plan for teaching someone how to ride a bike, especially someone who had failed and now was wholly unexcited about learning bike riding. Nonetheless, some of us work (or have worked) in schools where reading interventions have been designed to look a lot like this no-bike riding plan for developing bike riding proficiencies.

One good first step in thinking about any intervention design is to collect good data on how much reading the struggling readers do during both their classroom lessons and during the intervention reading lessons. "How to Measure Reading Volume" discusses several strategies to do just this. While collecting this information, you probably should also gather the same

How to Measure Reading Volume

When we want to examine the volume of reading, we have three possible measures that all work pretty well. We can simply record the time the student has spent reading, we can count the number of pages the student read, or we can count the number of words the student read. All three measures provide us with volume information and all three have been used in various studies of reading volume. Here are the strengths and weaknesses of all three approaches to gathering data on reading volume:

	Strengths	Weaknesses
Time spent reading	Simplest to gather	Some kids read faster
Number of pages read	More accurate than time	Some pages have more words
Number of words read	Most accurate	Takes more time to collect

I prefer gathering data on the number of words that were read because it seems to me to be the most reliable evidence, but I have also gathered both time spent reading and number of pages data as measures of reading volume. But when some students are reading 100 words per minute and others are reading 200, the data do not actually reflect the differences in reading volume. Likewise with pages read, because when struggling readers are reading a *Frog and Toad* book and the better readers are reading a *Junie B. Jones* book, the page totals do not adequately represent the differences in the number of words that were read. When we count (or estimate) the numbers of words that readers actually read, we get the most precise information on just how much reading practice has actually occurred.

The most efficient way to gather words read data is to use a words per line and lines per page method. Basically, the procedure you would use goes like this: (1) Select the text the student has been reading (noting, of course, which pages were read). (2) On any of the pages read, count the total number of words in 5 lines of typical print, and divide the number of words by 5. This gives you the typical average number of words per line on the pages. (3) Then count from 5 consecutive pages the number of lines of print on each page and divide by 5. This gives you the average number of lines per page. (4) Count the total number of pages read, and multiply that number by the average number of lines, and then multiply that number by the average number of words per line. This gives you the total number of words read.

information on the amount of reading being done by better readers during these same periods. Then ask: Is the intervention increasing the volume of reading that struggling readers do? Does the volume of reading the struggling readers are doing pretty much match the volume of reading the better readers are doing during the same periods?

Why Reading Volume Is Critical

Struggling readers need to read a lot because it is during the actual reading that they can practice all those complicated strategies and skills they are developing in unison. There is good evidence (Torgeson & Hudson, 2006) that we can design interventions that improve word recognition skills and strategies and still be left with students who cannot read fluently and with comprehension. It isn't that teaching struggling readers better word reading skills and strategies isn't important, but rather that better word reading skills and strategies will not necessarily improve the reading of text—real reading, the ultimate goal. What we need in order to help struggling readers develop is the substantially more complicated achievement of reading texts accurately, fluently, and with comprehension. The only way to do this is to design interventions such that struggling readers engage in lots of text reading.

To read texts fluently, with appropriate phrasing and expression, requires that students can read most of the words with little conscious effort. That means they don't have to slow down to sound out very many words. Most of the words they encounter will be those infamous at-a-glance words—words that are recognized in milliseconds, words that should not require much attention to pronounce.

The development of the at-a-glance words is largely a function of lots of high-success reading. The best information we have on how words become at-a-glance words (Adams, 1990) is that repeated, consecutive correct pronunciations of the word is required. That's why high-success reading is so critical and why reading volume is also.

Volume, however, goes well beyond developing at-a-glance words, to developing fluency, comprehension, and world knowledge. Melanie Kuhn and colleagues (2005, 2006) have recently demonstrated the advantages of having students engage in extensive reading. They compared a repeated reading intervention design with one where struggling readers did some repeated reading but spent most of their instructional time engaged in independent reading. They wrote,

> By the end of the school year, FORI [repeated reading] and wide-reading approaches showed similar benefits for standardized measures of word reading efficiency and reading comprehension compared to the control approaches, although the benefits of the wide-reading approach emerged earlier and included oral text reading fluency skill. (2006, p. 358)

What Do We Mean by Fluency?

In the past few years an assessment called DIBELS (Dynamic Indicators of Basic Early Literacy Skills) has become widely used in U.S. schools. This assessment system labels all its subtests as "fluency" tests, but none is. Instead, they are rate and accuracy tests. Although both reading accuracy and reading rate are related to fluency, they are not sufficient measures to replace fluency. As S. Jay Samuels (2007), the developer of automaticity theory, has noted:

> One criticism I have of the DIBELS tests is that, despite their labels, they are not valid tests of the construct of fluency as it is widely understood and defined. They only assess accuracy and speed. . . . By attaching the term *fluency* to their tests, they create the false assumption that that is what their tests measure. (p. 564)

So what is reading fluency? Most typically when researchers speak of reading fluency, they are speaking of the ability to do two things at once—reading the text with understanding. When the reading method is reading aloud, researchers use reading in phrases with appropriate expression as the definition of fluency. As Kuhn and Stahl (2003) noted in their review of over 100 studies of fluency:

> Given that fluent oral reading is considered to be expressive as well as quick and accurate and that prosodic features are, to a large extent, responsible for such expression, it is important to consider a definition of fluency that encompasses more than rate and accuracy. (p. 18)

So, it seems safe to conclude that reading volume fosters the development of reading fluency and text reading accuracy. That makes sense if only because practice improves fluency in the development of almost every human proficiency.

When it comes to comprehension while reading, volume is also critical. It is during high-success reading activity that readers have the opportunity to begin to consolidate all those separate reading skills and strategies (McGill-Franzen & Allington, 2008; Mastropieri & Scruggs, 1997). Implementing higher-order cognitive strategies such as summarizing, self-monitoring for understanding, implementing useful repair strategies, and others require that word recognition accuracy is high with low effort and that reading fluency is intact. With little high-success reading activity, none of these proficiencies develops. The lack of reading volume, especially high-success reading, explains why so many struggling readers struggle with these skills and strategies.

Research on Reading Volume during Interventions

In addition to the reasons just noted, which are largely based on theory, there is good research evidence to support ensuring that struggling readers must spend lots of time reading. In a series of intervention studies that have documented accelerated reading development as an outcome, roughly two-thirds of the intervention lessons involved having the students engage in high-success reading (Hiebert, Colt, Catto, & Gury, 1992; Mathes, Denton, Fletcher, Anthony, Francis, & Schatschneider, 2005; Pinnell, Lyons, DeFord, Bryk, & Seltzer, 1994; Scanlon, Vellutino, Small, Fanuele, & Sweeney, 2005; Vellutino, Sipay, Small, Pratt, Chen, & Denckla, 1996).

In each of these studies struggling readers spent approximately 20 minutes of every 30-minute intervention period engaged in high-success reading or writing. In many cases this equaled or exceeded the total volume of reading these struggling readers had done in their classroom reading lessons. The intervention design doubled the volume of reading that these struggling readers did every day. This doubling of reading volume was directly related to the accelerated reading growth.

So what do these intervention lessons look like? Typically, these were daily, small group lessons offered over a 30-minute period.

In each case the struggling readers were taught by certified teachers, often reading specialists. The reading activities were well matched to the children's needs and included both reading of new texts and rereading of some previously read texts. Roughly 5 minutes each day was assigned to developing useful decoding skills and strategies, and another 5 minutes was assigned to teaching and assessing understanding as illustrated in Figure 4.1.

Unfortunately, small group interventions are too often designed just opposite of this, with 20 minutes of teaching and 10 minutes of reading. I think it's because reading teachers and special education teachers feel the need to teach the kids everything they are not understanding, but the kids end up being taught all the time and are never allowed the necessary amount of practice, and most of them are not going to practice at home.

There are other intervention designs that produce reading growth, but those designs have not routinely produced accelerated reading growth—more than one year's growth per year on generalized reading achievement assessments. Instead, these intervention designs produce smaller amounts of growth in general reading achievement or growth only in some subcomponent of reading (e.g., phonological awareness, non-word decoding, word reading) but do not produce huge improvements in general reading achievement. As noted earlier, though, the new federal framework requires school districts to catch up struggling readers to their better reading peers, and that requires accelerated growth in general reading achievement.

I must note that all of the preceding intervention studies focused their efforts on primary-grade students (grades K–2). That is a problem if the

▶ Figure 4.1   **A research-based intervention design**

Daily 30-minute, expert, very small group intervention:

- 20 minutes of reading appropriate new texts and rereading previously read texts
- 5 minutes of word work or phonological skills work
- 5 minutes of work on comprehension skills and strategies

group being targeted for intervention is in fourth, sixth, or ninth grade. It is problematic because while there is no reason to suspect that a similar design wouldn't do the same for older students, by the upper elementary grades, many struggling readers are one, two, or even three years behind their achieving peers on reading development. What this means is that any intervention that lasts 30 minutes a day may need to be in place for multiple years, even if it is producing accelerated reading growth. One seldom used, or seldom studied, alternative is a longer daily, expert, small group intervention. It may be that we could double the amount of reading growth by doubling the amount of reading intervention time. That, of course, assumes that in a 60-minute daily reading intervention, students would more than double their volume of reading.

Showers, Joyce, Scanlon, and Schnaubelt (1998) found such outcomes for a high school reading intervention, at least for the majority of students. This was a reading intensive intervention design where the participating students read multiple books over the one or two semesters they took the special reading course offered in an urban high school. Currently, however, there are few intervention studies that include students above the primary grades, so the research base is simply much slimmer for older struggling readers. Nonetheless, the available evidence indicates two important findings: First, most older struggling readers have little, if any, opportunity to participate in any reading intervention. Second, when an intervention is available, it is likely not to be a reading intensive intervention. Instead, interventions for older struggling readers tend to be focused narrowly and typically involve very little full-text reading activity.

We can (and often do) design interventions that fail to even minimally increase reading volume. Instead, our interventions provide computerized vocabulary or phonemic awareness practice, or focus almost solely on developing decoding skills but add little text reading activity. These sorts of interventions have little evidence of producing accelerated reading growth. Instead, we observe smaller amounts of reading growth, say an added two months of reading growth. But that added two months of growth still allows the struggling readers to continue to fall behind, albeit at a slower loss rate than if that intervention was not available. For the past 50 or so years, almost everyone was satisfied with that outcome (except perhaps the struggling readers), but this is no longer the case.

If we are to attain the goal of all students reading proficiently, we will necessarily have to redesign the interventions we use. What will be absolutely critical is that in this redesign we must ensure that reading volume is dramatically increased if accelerated reading growth is the intended outcome.

How to Design Interventions That Dramatically Increase Reading Volume

The first aspect of redesigning current interventions to be reading intensive interventions is assuring that you have an adequate supply of texts that students find interesting and that they can read accurately, fluently, and with good understanding. Lots of books is not enough, however. But it is the beginning step—an absolutely necessary beginning.

Sufficient Supply of Books

The first step is documenting the number of appropriate texts that are available in your school. Start with the school library. Does the library meet or exceed the American Library Association's standards for adequacy? (You can locate information on these standards at www.ala.org/ala/ors/standardsa/ standardsguidelines/standguide.cfm.) In most schools the ALA standard is not met, and in far too many schools, there is no library available for students to use.

The second place to document ease of access that struggling readers have to appropriate and interesting texts is in the classrooms the students sit in all day. You might simply count the number of book titles available in each classroom. In most classrooms this is not a difficult problem because there are fewer than 200 titles available. Counting the number of different titles is one method, but it's not a very good method for estimating the number of texts that struggling readers can access and actually read accurately, fluently, and with understanding. To get a better estimate of these sorts of texts, you must look at each of the texts available in the classroom and judge whether the struggling readers in that classroom can read the titles independently. This

makes the task more difficult, but given the small number of titles in most rooms it is not an impossible task.

What you are looking for is classroom book collections that have hundreds of titles available, with many, say at least one-third, of the titles being at appropriate levels of difficulty that struggling readers can read them accurately, fluently, and with comprehension. Consider that if a first-grade student is engaged in reading at least 60 to 90 minutes every day, that means he or she must be reading (or rereading) roughly 5 to 10 books every day. Even if we use the low number (5) of books to estimate and we hope to double the amount of reading that struggling readers are doing (to 10 books a day), we will need hundreds of titles to supply the struggling readers with appropriate books all year long.

There are options that schools might consider to make easy access to appropriate books available for struggling readers. One that works especially well in the upper elementary-grade levels and into middle and high school is the rolling book bin. In my work in schools I have seen double-sided rolling book bins built to hold books in a portable container that is moved from classroom to classroom every week. This model works best when it is designed specifically for one particular grade level.

In such cases the book selection may be targeted to science and social studies state standards as well as to reading and language arts standards and student personal preferences. Linking the books available to other content areas works to ensure that struggling readers have materials available for science and social studies classes, something that helps getting struggling readers to read all day long (Allington, 2002b). It also works to increase the supply of informational texts that are available for struggling readers (and everyone else).

Access to appropriately difficult informational texts is critical, especially for struggling readers who too often cannot read the grade-level science textbook (or other grade-level science materials). When we examine current collections of tradebooks available in classrooms, we find not only that most classrooms have few books but also that most have almost no informational books and typically have none tied directly to the science or social studies standards (Duke, 2000; Guice, Allington, Johnston, Baker, & Michelson, 1996). American students are far better at reading stories (narrative texts) than they are at reading informational texts (Duke & Bennett-

Armistead, 2003). That seems largely the result of the neglect of informational text reading instruction that seems to be directly linked to the lack of available informational texts in most core reading programs. By providing a multilevel supply of informational texts tied to state content area standards, we can solve two problems: improving students' access to informational texts and improving the likelihood that struggling readers have books they can actually read in the content area instruction.

Some schools have developed book rooms where collections of books are available for units of study in content area instruction. In these schools, classroom teachers can check out multilevel bins of books for use to supplement the texts available in the classroom. In other schools, each teacher has multiple bins of books to use for science and social studies with each bin holding perhaps 30 to 50 different texts that students might use to learn social studies topics, for instance. These bins are also multilevel, containing texts across several levels of difficulty. However, such an approach is more expensive and requires more space in every classroom for storing these book bins.

Improving access of struggling readers to books they can actually read is critical to improving their reading growth (Allington, 2006a; Guthrie & Humenick, 2004; Reis, McCoach, Coyne, Schreiber, Eckert, & Gubbins, 2007; Shin & Krashen, 2008). In fact, Guthrie and Humenick conducted a meta-analysis—the same analytic procedure used by the National Reading Panel—on some 22 experimental or quasi-experimental studies of classroom reading instruction. They found a huge effect size (ES = 1.64) on reading comprehension achievement for ease of access students had to interesting texts. Just to understand the enormity of that effect size, it may be useful to know that it is four times as large as the effect size that the NRP found for systematic phonics instruction on word reading, and roughly ten times the size of the effect size phonics lessons had on reading comprehension. Easy access to interesting texts also had large positive effects on students' motivation to engage in reading.

So, ensuring that every classroom teacher has both access to a substantial number of multilevel texts and also has the expertise to use those texts productively across the school day is essential if we want to double the reading growth of struggling readers. It is also essential that every reading and special education teacher have access to this supply of texts for use during any intervention reading lessons he or she may be providing.

So, How Do You Buy So Many Books?

One question that I am always asked when I present these findings in schools is: So, how do you suggest we buy all these books? My answer is: It depends on your school and who works there primarily. To create such large collections of appropriate texts, especially collections linked to science and social studies standards, will require some people who know a lot about the books in these areas. In virtually every school system such experts are available, and where they are not, there exists other options, such as using outside consultants or working with employees of book vendors such as Scholastic, the Book Source, Barnes & Noble, Borders, Books-A-Million, and others. But whoever is charged with selecting the books should be wary of trying to order books from catalogs alone or from buying standard collections that some vendors have available.

Build into your book-purchasing plan a minimum of a three-year period for building the collection of books, and ensure the plan is designed to allow the continued updating of the collection. In my work with schools I suggest that over the three-year period expect to purchase 20 percent, 30 percent, and 50 percent of the total collection in years 1, 2, and 3. The reason for this is that people get better at selecting texts with practice, and in most schools no one is very expert at first. And do not allow the folks purchasing the books to forget that the major reason for acquiring this variety of texts is to provide sufficient texts that struggling readers can read. Thus, everyone needs to be concerned with the difficulty of the books being purchased.

Where Will the Money Come From to Buy All These Books?

This is another good question and one with multiple answers. In North America there are no schools that are resource deprived. Every school has the funding available to create these book collections. In many cases that money is currently being spent on other things—usually things that are not supported by the research.

In one southern school the principal decided to create a money supply simply by eliminating all consumable products from her purchases. By eliminating funds for items such as workbooks, including test preparation materials, all the money that the school needed to dramatically increase the number of books in the classrooms and school library became available. We find that lower-achieving schools spend enormous sums of money on consumable materials, even though there is no research that supports the use of such materials (Allington & Nowak, 2004; Jachym, Allington, & Broikou, 1989). We found some lower-achieving schools that spent as much as $300 per student on consumables (including copying costs). With that kind of money being spent on books, we could purchase roughly 100 books for every student in the school, every year! The point is that whenever there is a will to begin to develop a large collection of multilevel texts, there is a way to fund those purchases. But usually it also means giving up something.

In other schools, the money allocated to purchasing new textbooks has been used to create large collections of multilevel texts. States differ in how textbook dollars can be spent, but in every state there is a way to purchase something other than traditional one-size-fits-all textbooks with that money. Spending textbook dollars for such purchases has the additional benefit of directly pointing out to teachers that not only is the sole use of a standard textbook not required but it is also not advised. However, many teachers will need much support to learn how to best use a multilevel and multisourced curriculum.

In addition to consumable and textbook dollars in many districts there are other money options as well to purchase the books that will be needed. In some cases there are special state funds for innovative projects (e.g., Title I programs) that can be used to purchase the books needed. In other cases, there are local district funds that could be used as well. In the classrooms of the exemplary teachers we studied we almost always recorded huge numbers of texts available, and in most cases these individual teachers had begged, borrowed, and bought these texts (Allington & Johnston, 2002; Pressley et al., 2001). These teachers had used PTA funds, reading council funds, Title I funds, special education funds, and so on to build their multilevel book collections over the years.

To begin, then, you must first decide that ease of access to multiple appropriate texts is important, and then you can begin asking where the funds will come from. I don't think individual teachers should be expected to spend their own funds to purchase the books they will need for an intervention design that will make it far easier for struggling readers to have books they can read in their rooms and in their hands all day long. That is the responsibility of the school district that employs them.

Summary

High-success reading is one of the essential components of any intervention designed to accelerate reading development. In most schools, easy access to high-success texts is in short supply for struggling readers. We can and must do better on this factor.

Struggling readers need easy access to a huge supply of books they can read accurately, fluently, and with understanding. They also need lots of books they cannot wait to read. There is an enormous supply of such books available, though not typically from the companies that supply schools. This means that schools need to develop a plan for the acquisition of the books that are needed, books often available outside the normal sources of supply. A three-year plan for acquiring the needed books is essential, along with a plan for supporting the continued updating of the collection you have, once it is developed.

chapter 5

Using Very Small Groups or Tutoring

There is another problem with the current design of most reading intervention programs: The size of the instructional groups is simply too large.

The evidence available indicates that expecting accelerated reading growth to be produced with a large group of struggling readers is but a pipe dream. In my evaluation of the accelerated reading growth intervention research, I found no studies that worked with groups as large as those currently in place in remedial reading or special education interventions. The studies using one-to-one tutoring produced the most consistently reliable accelerated reading growth. Models using very small group intervention designs, groups no larger than 3, followed close on the heels of the tutoring models. So, in the redesign of current intervention programs, we will need to begin to address the problem of too many struggling readers in the intervention groups.

Research on Intervention Group Size

We know a lot about the size of typical intervention groups. The federal study of Title I programs (Puma, Karweit, Price, Ricciuti, Thompson, & Vaden-Kiernan, 1997), for instance, found that groups of 5 to 9 students were the most common but with still many schools offering intervention services in larger groups and only a very few schools providing one-to-one tutoring or even very small-sized intervention group lessons. As for special education, group sizes were roughly the same size as Title I program groups (Vaughn, Linan-Thompso, Kouzekanani, Bryant, Dickson, & Blozis, 2003).

Puma and colleagues (1997) noted that federal Title I funds have long been spread broadly but thinly across virtually every school district in the United States. They found that Title I intervention services added one or two months of additional reading growth each year struggling readers were provided services. At the same time, they argued that "the level of instructional assistance Title I students generally received was in stark contrast to their levels of educational need" (p. iii). In other words, the federal Title I program provided services to only some of the students who were eligible, and typically those services were modest, at best. One result of these limitations was limited reading growth among participating students.

Borman and D'Agostino (2001) analyzed federal data to estimate the size of the reading growth produced in Title I interventions as well. The evidence indicates that Title I effects have grown across the years since the 1980s compared to a finding of no effects in the earliest analysis of program effects. They similarly concluded: "This pattern of improvement suggests that once the program was effectively implemented . . . the effects reached a peak that has not changed substantially. . . . This result could suggest that an effect size of .15 is the best that can be done given the current federal funding commitment" (pp. 51–52).

However, both of these research teams seem to be suggesting that the federal money available through the Title I legislation (No Child Left Behind) should provide sufficient dollars to purchase greater levels of service. Perhaps, but I would argue that the education of struggling readers is primarily the responsibility of local taxpayers, not the responsibility of the federal government. The fact that the federal government sends local education agencies federal dollars to fund some intervention services should be viewed positively. But I do not assume that the writers of the federal laws that allocate these funds intended all intervention services that were needed would be funded by those laws. In fact, the earliest versions of the law that funds Title I programs required matching local dollars for every federal dollar received. However, because some school districts then decided not to apply for these federal dollars, Congress ultimately changed the law to create the current policy that has no matching funds requirements (Allington, 2002a).

Intervention reading services provided under federal special education laws are far less researched than other federal efforts. Nonetheless, as a number of researchers have noted (Jenkins, Pious, & Peterson, 1988; Johnston & Allington, 1990; Thurlow, Ysseldyke, Wotruba, & Algozzine, 1993; Vaughn et al., 2003), the sizes of the groups of struggling readers served in special education resource room programs varies enormously, as different states offer quite different guidelines on this topic. Again, however, very few pupils with disabilities seem to be provided either one-to-one tutoring or very small group intervention reading lessons in special education settings that the research suggests is optimal.

The reading growth of students receiving special education services is not well documented. Until 2002 and the adequate yearly progress requirements of NCLB, there was virtually no national data on this issue. It wasn't until the Individuals with Disabilities Education Act (IDEA) was reauthorized in 1998 that pupils with disabilities even sat for state reading assessments. That reauthorization made participation in state and national reading assessments a requirement for pupils with disabilities. But while the reading outcomes data are now beginning to appear, there are significant problems with those national data.

The problem primarily lies in the IDEA's allowance for local committees on special education to adapt or modify the delivery of the state assessments. Thus, we have some states where reading the state reading assessment aloud to pupils with disabilities is allowed, and some states where the same modification is a punishable violation of the rules, and, finally, some states where teachers can read the proper nouns in the test aloud but not the rest of the reading test. I have recently lived in two of the states that ban reading a reading test to any student (New York and Florida) and now live in a state where reading the test to pupils with disabilities is allowed and popular (Tennessee). Not surprisingly, the state of Tennessee reports much higher percentages of pupils with disabilities meeting the state reading standards than the other two states. But almost none of those pupils with disabilities in Tennessee who pass the state reading test can actually read (McGill-Franzen & Allington, 2006).

The primary point to all this is: There is little evidence that many schools currently provide tutorial or very small group reading interventions for struggling readers. I will simply suggest that this is another critical factor in the failure of most school district reading interventions to catch up struggling readers with their achieving peers.

The Research on Interventions That Accelerate Reading Growth

If we look at the evidence that is available from the Swanson and Hoskyn meta-analysis (1998) of over 900 reading/learning disability intervention studies, we see that smaller intervention groups was one of the three factors that explained reading growth. When we examine the most successful interventions available in the research, we find that virtually every study used either one-to-one tutorial or very small group (1 to 3 students) lesson designs. Likewise, when we examine what other researchers have written about effective intervention designs, we find a near unanimous agreement that very small instructional groups or tutorials are needed (Allington, 2006c; Denton, Vaughn, & Fletcher, 2003; Foorman & Torgeson, 2001; Fuchs & Fuchs, 2005; McEneaney, Lose, & Schwartz, 2006). In fact, Denton and colleagues concluded their review of this research by noting: "Research on grouping reveals that pull-out programs typically consist of group sizes that are too large and provide insufficient intensity to meet the specific needs of students" (p. 204).

Examining the data in Table 5.1 illustrates the issue of intervention group size in the most effective intervention research studies. As is easily seen, each of these research teams used either tutorials or very small group intervention designs. Although each was successful in producing accelerated reading growth, on average, not every struggling reader in these studies was caught up to peers nor did everyone make accelerated progress. Torgeson (2000) addresses this issue across a number of studies as well, and notes that in those studies anywhere from 12 to 40 percent of the struggling readers did not benefit much from the intervention lessons. Such treatment failures, even when most of the struggling readers did make accelerated reading growth, give us cause for concern. In some cases the problem may lie with the student (e.g., limited intellectual abilities, child abuse, or attendance issues). But in most cases the problem lies in the treatment. In other words, many intervention

▶ Table 5.1 **Size of Intervention Groups in Effective Intervention Research**

	Teacher/Student Ratio
Ehri et al., 2007	1 to 1
Lyons & Beaver, 1995	1 to 1
Pinnell et al., 1994	1 to 1
Scanlon et al., 2005	1 to 1
Torgeson et al., 2001	1 to 1
Vellutino et al., 1996	1 to 1
Hiebert et al., 1992	1 to 3
Mathes et al., 2005	1 to 3

studies have selected an intervention design that was not well suited for some of the participating students.

This is another issue that we must always attend to: Is this the correct intervention design for this particular struggling reader? If little reading growth is being observed, consideration of an intervention redesign is needed. That redesign might add intervention instructional time, reduce the group size further, refocus the lesson content, and so on. But something must be redesigned so that accelerated reading development is observed.

Why Very Small Intervention Groups Are Necessary

It is difficult to find a classroom teacher who would argue that having 30 students in a class is far better than having 15 students in a class. Likewise, it is impossible to find research that indicates that academic outcomes for students improve when there are 30 students versus 15 students in a class. In fact, the research on class size is quite clear: Smaller classes, say 15 students, produce superior outcomes when compared to larger classes, say 25 or more students, or even when compared to larger classes with a full-time teaching assistant (Achilles, 1999; Finn & Achilles, 1990).

When it comes to intervention groups, however, there has been far less experimental research where the size of the group was manipulated. Nonetheless, Elbaum, Vaughn, Hughes, and Moody (2000) conducted a meta-analysis to examine the reported effect of different intervention group sizes on academic outcomes. Not surprisingly, they found that smaller groups produced better achievement growth. But there is one significant issue involved in determining the effectiveness of differently sized groups that they largely overlooked. This is the *number* of students who are well served versus the *proportion* of students who are well served.

My analysis of the research, for instance, on the effects of very small group interventions versus one-to-one tutoring interventions indicates that the former accelerates the development of a larger number of students while the latter accelerates the development of a larger proportion of students. Think of the issue as one of looking at the overall outcomes of a very small group (1 to 3 children) reading intervention versus a one-to-one intervention design. If we assume the teachers in each model deliver reading instruction for 5 hours each day and that both are working with their students in 30-minute sessions, then the 1-to-3 teachers work with 30 struggling readers each day and the 1-to-1 teachers work with 10 students. Imagine the very small group teacher accelerates the reading development of two-thirds of her students such that they are caught up to their peers, and the tutorial teacher accelerates the development of 80 percent of her students so that they are caught up. If we examine only the proportion of students who have their reading development accelerated, then the tutorial model works quite a bit better than the very small group model. But if we examine the numbers of struggling readers whose reading growth was accelerated and who caught up to their peers, then the very small group model wins the comparison 20 students to 8.

Another way to examine this same issue is to design a study where the group size is systematically varied for struggling readers. This is just what Vaughn and colleagues (2003) did. They compared interventions with 1-to-1 tutorial instruction, 1-to-3 very small groups, and 1-to-10 large intervention groups. They found that 7, 20, and 33 percent, respectively, of the struggling readers in these groups failed to benefit much from the various group sizes. But this is one of very few such studies available in the research, and thus these percentages cannot be viewed as terrifically reliable estimates of the usual failure rates. Nonetheless, the study provides good evidence that similar intervention lessons offered in different-sized instructional groups will be differentially effective at promoting reading growth.

The size of the intervention groups is not a trivial issue. When educational dollars are not available to fully support tutorial models, we must consider such outcomes. I will suggest that when we design our intervention efforts, we develop a plan that initiates intervention with very small group intervention lessons and then move students whose reading growth is not accelerated sufficiently into tutorial lessons. Just when to make this decision is largely a local decision, but it seems to me that if after 10 or 12 weeks of very small group lessons, we observe that some struggling readers are not developing their reading proficiencies satisfactorily, we need to consider moving those students to tutorial lesson designs.

In an ideal world we would select the students for the very small group intervention lessons such that struggling readers with similar instructional levels and needs were attending together. One reason very small groups work better than larger groups is that by having only three students, the variance in reading levels and needs is typically smaller than when we have nine students attending the same intervention lesson. Thus, the reading intervention lesson can be designed such that a greater number of students benefit and far fewer students continue to struggle. We can work to better assure similar instructional levels and needs and make it more likely that the very small group lessons produce improved reading growth.

Scheduling Small Group and Tutorial Intervention Lessons

As far as the research is concerned, most effective intervention programs provide, minimally, daily 30-minute very small group intervention lessons. For this reason, I would recommend the same. Remember that the goal is accelerated reading growth and that all reading growth is linked to the amount of high-success reading that students actually do. Thus, the 150 minutes of intervention lessons provided in the daily 30-minute periods is simply greater than the 90 minutes provided with the twice weekly 45-minute lesson design. However, having made the argument for the daily 30-minute very small group design, I must note that an every other day 45-minute very small group design seems more powerful than the larger intervention groups coming daily for 30 minutes design.

Scheduling Intervention Lessons

When should the intervention lessons be scheduled during the school day? If we want to add instructional minutes to the struggling reader's school day, and we do, then the intervention lessons must be scheduled outside the classroom reading block. This is another serious aspect of intervention program design. Central to the design of effective interventions is the addition of reading instruction and practice time. If we simply replace some of the classroom reading lesson with the intervention lesson, we add no new minutes of instructional time. If we add no new minutes of instructional time, there is little reason to expect that we will obtain accelerated reading growth.

In too many schools today, though, whatever intervention is provided occurs during the classroom reading time. This is often done in an attempt to ensure that struggling readers are in the classroom during math, science, and social studies lessons and so that struggling readers do not miss participating in music, art, and physical education or library periods. Certainly, missing content area or other classes is not easy to recommend, but if accelerated growth in reading is to be an outcome of intervention lessons, then missing something offered outside of the classroom reading lessons is going to be required unless we move the intervention into an after-school program design.

One way to decide what will be missed in the classroom in order to deliver very small group intervention lessons is to consider which other lesson the struggling reader is most capable and interested in. In some schools the regular use of a grade-level textbook in science or social studies means that struggling readers typically cannot read those texts, so participation in those lessons is often problematic. In such cases I would argue those are the lessons to be missed. If we are concerned about the learning of social studies or science content, we can always design the intervention lessons around that content.

For instance, in many states' social studies standards for fourth grade there is a requirement that aspects of state history and geography be learned. We can design effective reading interventions focused on that social studies content if we want to. The basic alteration would be the selection of texts that cover that content and that are appropriate for the struggling readers. Likewise, we can do the same with third-grade science standards or fifth-grade health standards. I worry that we have been too little concerned about what struggling readers might be learning during intervention lessons besides learning to read. Greater attention to this provides us with one solution to the problem of fourth-grade struggling readers being scheduled for intervention lessons during classroom science or social studies lessons.

This would also be a concern if we elected to provide all, or some, struggling readers with intervention support in an after-school program (such as is now required through the federal Supplementary Educational Services provisions of NCLB). Rather than leave the "What is to be learned?" question unaddressed, I think all schools should consider this issue in the design of any intervention program. It isn't the case that the intervention design needs to elect to focus on a single content area or genre but rather that we always ask ourselves: What will struggling readers be learning while they are learning to read?

In the end, the issue of scheduling intervention lessons has been too little addressed. Too often the schedules we have created were focused more on what was convenient for classroom teachers and less on basic research-based design principles. What we need are very small group intervention lessons scheduled such that the amount of reading instruction and the volume of reading practice are both extended every day for struggling readers.

Funding Small Group and Tutorial Intervention Lessons

There are federal, state, and local resources available to provide the funding needed to offer very small group intervention lessons to every struggling reader. These resources vary from school to school even within a school district. Thus, this section is written quite broadly, and not every potential resource will be available for every school.

Special Education Funding

The most obvious place to locate funding, at least to begin interventions, is the 15 percent of your school's special education funding that can be allocated to support response to intervention initiatives. States vary in just how this money can be tapped but federal law has allocated such funding since 2004. Even though special education funds are being used, all response to intervention models are considered general education initiatives (Zirkel, 2006; National Association of State Directors of Special Education, 2006, available at www.nasdse.org). Given that on a national level the typical additional funding available for each special education student is in the $5,000 to $7,000 range, in many schools this special funding can go a long way in supporting intensive, expert reading interventions.

In addition to the special education RTI funding possibility there is also a chance that all the funding available for special education student support could be used to fund the interventions offered to pupils with disabilities. Since these struggling readers are now part of the adequate yearly progress subgroups, accelerating their reading growth is now required. In such a case it is a redesigning of current special education services into intensive, very small group interventions.

A similar situation exists in schools where federal Title I or Reading First funds are available to support supplementary educational services for struggling readers. After special education funding, in most schools these programs provide the greatest pools of potential funding. The redesign of remedial reading interventions into intensive, very small group interventions is another of the essential ideas if we are planning to accelerate the reading development of struggling learners.

Some states also provide excess funding to address the needs of struggling readers, and these programs vary widely and are not available in all states. However, when such funds are available, it is possible that a state will fund intensive, very small group intervention programs.

In the end, though, many schools will be required to do something most have never done. These schools (and districts) will have to raise local educational funds to support research-based interventions in order to meet the federal adequate yearly progress standards. I say this because although there are options that might make this unnecessary, most of those options will not be selected and most schools currently allocate insufficient funding to support the sorts of intervention designs that will accelerate reading development and help struggling readers catch up with their achieving peers.

You may be wondering about those options I said were unlikely to be selected. Here is my argument for how to use existing resources to provide what struggling readers need. It is an argument that has been routinely ignored or rejected when presented to schools or districts. Nonetheless, I argue that virtually every school and district I visit already has sufficient adults to provide all of the needed tutorial and very small group reading interventions. However, most of the adult employees in any school or district are not teachers who deliver direct instructional services to students. In the district I visited last week there were two other adults in every elementary school building for each classroom teacher there. Roughly half of the adults were certified professionals (e.g., principals and assistant principals; guidance counselors;

school psychologists; librarians; special education, remedial reading, gifted, and ESL teachers; speech and language pathologists; physical therapists; computer specialists; home/school attendance officer; and so on). In addition, each building had more paraprofessional adults than classroom teachers. Finally, in this district there were central administration staff (e.g., superintendent and assistant superintendents, curriculum supervisors, federal programs administrator, special education director, ESL director, professional development personnel, athletic director, and so on) as well. My point is that there are more than enough adults already employed in your school and district to provide every single struggling reader with very small group intervention lessons. However, someone would have to decide that access to very small group interventions was an important option. Someone would necessarily have to redesign some of these positions such that delivering very small group intervention services was part of every single employee's job, even if only part of the job (say two 30-minute periods each day).

A similar situation exists in many schools, and someone could redesign the job descriptions of all employees such that everyone provided some very small group intervention every day. Everyone, including the superintendent, would work with struggling learners, every day. But so far, this argument has not been accepted with any sort of openness in any of the schools I've visited. You might propose this option in your school or district, but don't be surprised if no one says, "Of course" and redesigns professional roles.

Perhaps at the school level, though, we could work to ensure something similar took place. It's easier in the smaller unit of the school. There are schools where everyone works in a tutorial or very small intervention group mode every day, before or after school begins or ends. Imagine the number of very small intervention groups that could be added to your school if every adult in the building worked both before and after school every day with one intervention group. According to federal data, there are currently three different lengths of the school day. In a substantial number of schools, students attend for 6, 6½, or 7 hours every day (of course there a few schools with both longer and shorter days). Oddly, it is students of color and poor students who attend schools with the shortest school days, and middle-class white students who attend the longest school days. In these data, the longer school days produced added instructional time (Roth, Brooks-Dunn, Linver, & Hofferth, 2002).

However, in each of these most popular school day lengths, there is at least 1½ hours every day (and in some schools 2½ to 3 hours every day) when teachers are in the building but not working with students (assuming an 8½-hour work day for teachers). It is during these periods that the schools I've observed have provided their struggling readers (before and/or after school intervention) with services and support. In every school I've been in that provides this sort of service, the principal is working with students in his or her own very small groups. Classroom teachers often work with students from their own classrooms that need the extra support. Specialist teachers work with struggling readers from across the classrooms. Many of the struggling readers who participate get only these services and so are in their general education classrooms all day long. In other words, they do not miss any of the general education curriculum or instruction.

Flextime

In some schools the use of flextime teacher schedules is well established for providing some struggling readers with intervention support before and/or after school. By flextime, I mean different teachers work different schedules so as to provide before- or after-school instruction. If school begins at 8:30 and ends at 3:30, then some specialist teachers work a 9:30 to 4:30 schedule in order to provide very small group lessons to two groups of struggling readers every day after school (Allington & Cunningham, 2006). There are many ways to do flextime schedules, but the point is to use them to create additional opportunities for every struggling reader to participate in very small group interventions.

Whenever I discuss before- and after-school intervention designs I'm typically told that student transportation is the problem even in schools where everyone walks to school! I will admit that moving students outside the official district bus schedule can be a problem. But it is a problem that almost never undermines the school day programs I've observed. Most parents will go out of their way to arrange to get their struggling readers to school early or to come and pick them up late if those students are getting high-quality instructional services. In many school districts there is already a transportation option that allows high school athletes a bus ride home after scheduled practices, so someone in the district has already created a model to emulate. The point is that we can create a transportation problem or we can address and solve this problem.

Summary

As currently structured, most interventions for struggling readers provide intervention lessons to groups too large to expect accelerated reading growth. The research available on effective reading interventions does not hold out much hope for any intervention group larger than three struggling readers. Ideally, all three should have similar instructional levels and needs. We already have enough certified adults in most schools to provide every struggling reader with very small group intervention instruction, but redesigning the professional roles of each of those adults such that everyone offers at least two intervention lessons every day has not been a popular idea. We might also restructure the school day so that every school offers before- and after-school intervention lessons through role redesign or flextime scheduling or both. Transportation for students who attend these before- and after-school programs can be a problem, but that problem is not insurmountable. Someone needs to step up, take on the problem, and find the solutions that will work for the student population.

We can continue to provide reading intervention lessons to groups too large to expect accelerated reading growth or we can begin to redesign our efforts to ensure every struggling gets daily, intensive, very small group support.

chapter 6
Coordinating Intervention with Core Classroom

W̲hat should intervention lessons look like? There is a simple though often ignored answer—a research-based answer. That is, intervention lesson design should take its cues from the classroom instruction.

The evidence available suggests that the vast majority of struggling readers receive interventions that are not informed by classroom lessons. That is another reason why accelerated reading growth too often is not an intervention outcome. The linking of classroom reading lessons and intervention reading lessons can be a tricky matter. In this chapter I review the research on the nature of intervention lessons and their links, if any, to the classroom curriculum and instruction. Then I discuss how better coordination of lessons can be developed and how to build the shared knowledge that is essential in designing interventions for struggling readers.

What Research Says about Intervention Lesson Design and Links to the Classroom Lessons

There are basically only two studies of the links between classroom and intervention lessons. One study was done 20 years ago; the other is more recent. Johnston, Allington, and Afflerbach (1985) studied intervention programs in 10 school districts located in two states. In this study both the classroom teacher and the intervention teacher who worked with the same struggling readers were interviewed. The interview questions focused on the struggling reader and the reading instruction offered by the two teachers for that student. We found that far more students experienced curricular conflict than curricular coordination in the classroom and intervention settings. *Curricular conflict* occurs when the two curricula have competing philosophies and strategy lessons. *Curricular coordination* occurs when the two curricula appear to support similar philosophies of reading and similar strategy use.

In this particular study a common curriculum strategy conflict was observed between a classroom reading program that emphasized the use of the initial consonant and textual context while reading to monitor reading sense and an intervention curriculum where the words were all decodable and context was just not emphasized but rather largely eliminated. When struggling readers were taught in both of these programs, they experienced curriculum strategy conflict because the two sets of instructional materials and lessons were designed from very different philosophical bases.

Likewise, when word pronunciation is taught quite differently in the two settings, say synthetic phonics versus onset-rime approaches, it is difficult to see how lessons can be well coordinated and how students can ever figure out word decoding strategies. When the classroom teacher has much teacher-directed work in his or her lesson (guided reading and lots of worksheets), then you probably can't expect the struggling readers to function well in a student-directed curriculum (self-selected independent reading and discussions with peers) in the other setting. The case is the same when one set of lessons focuses on skills instruction in isolation and the other on independent use of reading strategies. In addition, what is being learned in one setting is not typically transferable to the other setting. The struggling readers could not use strategies in both instructional materials. They had to develop a reading mindset that allowed them to adjust strategy use depending on which instructional setting they were in. Struggling readers must develop schizophrenic tendencies just to survive in these uncoordinated reading programs. We argued that such situations did not benefit struggling readers.

We also found that two-thirds of the specialist teachers were unable to identify the reading instructional materials their students were using in the regular classroom. Fewer than one in ten classroom teachers could name the materials or method used in the intervention setting. This lack of shared knowledge of the reading lessons offered in the two settings cannot bode well for coordinated reading instruction. In fact, we found only a very few examples of any coordination in our study. The vastly dominant instructional model was one that created curricular and strategy conflicts for struggling readers.

As a result of our findings, we hypothesized that the lack of coordination was one of the reasons few interventions produced very many struggling readers who made accelerated reading progress. Instead, we argued, the very design of the two sets of reading lessons seemed more likely to develop confused readers than thoughtful readers. The dominant design we found seemed more likely to develop struggling readers who obtained partial knowledge of multiple strategies and full and consistent use of none.

Using our evidence as a basis, Borman, Wong, Hedges, and D'Agostino (2003) reanalyzed data from the federal Prospects study of Title I remediation services. These data were from 4,228 Title I students and questionnaires completed by their Title I and classroom teachers. They used a two-level hierarchical model analysis to predict reading achievement effects of curricular coordination and found that increases in coordination were

> associated with an increase of 4.7 to 7.1 normal curve equivalents in classroom mean reading achievement . . . and with a reduction of the Title I achievement gap by 0.2 to 0.3 standard deviation units. In other words, when Title I and regular teachers implement a curriculum that is similar or the same, they may increase the achievement levels of all students, and may reduce a substantial proportion of Title I students' achievement deficits. (p. 112)

Additionally, curriculum coordination was the only one of the eight variables they studied that achieved statistical significance. Borman and colleagues concluded that what matters is that the intervention teachers and the classroom teachers both use

> the same curriculum and assessments for all students. If the intervention coursework is not the same, there must be some articulation of how it will reinforce and complement the students' learning of the regular classroom curriculum. (p. 113)

In short, then, curriculum coordination is an important, though often overlooked, aspect of designing interventions that accelerate reading growth.

At the same time, Borman and colleagues (2003) also reported that approximately seven of ten intervention programs evidenced little coordination, and coordination was unrelated to other aspects of how the intervention program were organized. They found no difference in size of the effect of coordination when interventions were offered in the general education classroom than when the design pulled struggling readers from their classrooms to a different location for intervention services.

The research on location of the delivery of intervention services is replete with contradictory evidence (Archambault,

1989). Archambault's conclusion after reviewing the various studies available suggest: "Based on what we know, it is safe to conclude that setting is not directly responsible for student outcomes and that the issue of effective practices within settings, and not the setting itself, should be the focus of our attention" (p. 255). No new evidence of larger effects for one setting option (in-class, pullout, or a combination of these) has been presented since Archambault's comprehensive review of the research. Thus, his advice to focus on effective practices seems to be valid. This assumes, though, that the interventions actually expand both the reading instructional time and actual reading activity within a coordinated curricular framework.

Of course, like most educational issues, curriculum coordination can be difficult to achieve for many reasons. It is these reasons that are addressed in the next section.

Problems Associated with Defining Curriculum Coordination

A good first question to ask is: Why have most intervention efforts in schools so rarely included curriculum coordination in their design? It seems that several factors can account for this lack of coordination. First, federal rules and regulations for the expenditure of federal money in Title I, special education, and even in programs for English language learners have all required that new and specialized services for the intended student populations be purchased. Perhaps the best way to exhibit this was to employ special teachers working with different instructional materials in a setting different from the general education classroom. Second, most university programs that prepared the specialized teachers who worked in these intervention programs educated groups of teachers from multiple school districts, and the instruction they provided focused almost solely on determining individual student needs with little attention to local school district curricula. The third problem is the role definition associated with the special teachers who provided the interventions. One good way to present this new role in schools was to use different curriculum materials, especially curriculum materials published specifically for use in intervention efforts. Finally, there is the issue that whatever the general education curriculum, struggling readers were obviously not benefiting much from its use, so trying an alternative curriculum seemed a logical option. My hunch is that all of these factors had some influence in virtually every school and, in the end, intervention design ignored the potential of curriculum coordination.

The evidence now available indicates that ignoring curriculum coordination comes with some risk. That risk is less student growth in reading when compared to coordinated reading instruction. But we must, as a first step, attempt to define curriculum coordination between the classroom and intervention reading instruction. Here, I will discuss curriculum coordination from three perspectives: school, district, and state.

School

As already noted, when the classroom and intervention lessons provided in a variety of schools were studied, little evidence of coordinated reading lessons was found. But some schools were also found where coordination of the instruction was evident. What was it about these schools that accounted for the coordination? In most cases it was individual effort, usually by intervention teachers. In other words, intervention teachers worked, on their own initiative, to create reading instruction that extended and intensified the classroom reading lessons. We did find at least one school where the school administrator played just such a role also. In this case it was her efforts that led the classroom and specialist teachers to work toward better shared knowledge of struggling readers and better coordination of the reading instruction offered by these teachers.

District

We found no school districts in the original study that worked to develop coordination, but in later studies (Allington & Johnston, 1989) such efforts were described. In each case some district-level school administrator had developed district policies that emphasized a coordinated effort and in most cases had fostered greater communication between classroom and intervention teachers. However, in that report we also noted problematic aspects of fragmentation identified by the district administrators:

- The method used to control text difficulty in differing beginning materials: Word frequency vs. decodability vs. predictability.
- Strategies to be taught/learned differed in the different settings/materials: Use of initial consonant and context vs. sound out each letter and blend into a word.
- Instructional techniques differed in the different settings: Teacher vs. student directed school tasks.
- Terminology and metaphors differed such as when use of onset-rime approach to phonics competes with synthetic sound and blend approach.
- The presumed hierarchy of learning differed, as when one setting emphasized oral reading speed and accuracy and the other emphasized self-regulated reading with comprehension.
- Longstanding beliefs about teacher control of instruction such that both teachers believed that they were responsible for selecting the reading curricula they would be using. (Allington & Johnston, 1989, pp. 332–333)

Each of these six factors worked against coordinated reading lessons and, luckily, no district seemed to have problems with all six of the factors. How district administrators worked to foster better coordination is the topic of the next section, but work they did.

State and Federal Education Policies

As noted earlier, some state or federal rules and regulations seemed to work against coordination. The most common was the federal "supplement not supplant" regulation. Basically, this regulation stipulated that federal funds be

spent only on services that supplemented the educational services that were already being provided to students in the district. In effect, then, federal funds were not to be used to supplant, or replace, local educational services. The best illustration of this principle is when the intervention lesson is provided to struggling readers.

The federal rule (still in effect) literally would bar reading intervention services during the classroom reading block. That is because if students were pulled out of their classroom during the general education reading block, the intervention would be supplanting, or replacing, reading lessons that would be provided were the federal funds not available. However, even with this federal rule, the most common time for reading intervention instruction remains during the classroom reading block (Puma et al., 1997). But such designs are not just illegal; they are also shortsighted because they ensure that the intervention adds no reading instructional time to the struggling reader's school day.

An additional problem that exists in some states, particularly the few states where textbook adoptions are still run as a statewide initiative, is the state education agencies' listing of specific curriculum materials that schools may purchase with intervention funding. Such policies invariably present sets of instructional materials for use in remedial and special education programs that are different from those used in the classrooms, and I know of no state with such policies where curriculum coordination is even on the agenda. Thus, in these states, literally by state mandate, we find uncoordinated reading lessons in the general education and the intervention classrooms.

A few states have, over the years, attempted to mandate greater coordination of the reading lessons offered to struggling readers, but because of the complexity of the issue, there is no real research record of whether these efforts have been successful. Nonetheless, it is my view that working to develop state and federal policies that enhance coordinated reading instruction should be developed.

The research indicates that we have long designed intervention instruction to be different, often very different, from the classroom reading instruction that struggling readers receive. There are many reasons for this outcome, but the research also shows that uncoordinated programs work far less well than more coordinated reading instruction, at least if accelerated reading growth is the goal.

Different Beginning Reading Materials

Text difficulty can be judged using different methods, and using different methods produces different estimates of difficulty (Hiebert, 2002). In beginning reading materials we can find three distinct measures of organizing text difficulty. The oldest and still common method for controlling text difficulty is based on the number of *high-frequency words* in the text. The more high-frequency words, the lower the difficulty of the text. The second method involves organizing texts so that all (or almost all) words used are *decodable,* given the decoding abilities of the reader. The greater the number of decodable words, the lower the difficulty. The third organizes texts around *predictability, repetition,* and *rhyming.* Here, texts that feature repetitive sentence structures along with high levels of predictability and rhyme are considered the easiest texts.

These different methods for creating easier texts result not only in texts that do not much look like each other but also in texts that are harder or easier, depending on the nature of the classroom reading texts and lessons. With a common reading assessment system, such as running records, it will be possible to have discussions about which strategies students are using and which they are not. That is a basis for designing an intervention lesson. Without the running record data though, teachers may find discussions of student needs difficult, if not impossible, to do because they may have little shared knowledge.

Enhancing Curriculum Coordination in Schools

One of the things the research indicates is that simply mandating coordination of reading lessons may be a useful initial step, but even then the results are likely to be unsatisfactory (Allington & Johnston, 1989). I think it is the complexity of the issue of coordination and the longstanding uncoordinated designs that largely stand in the way of better linking of the reading instruction in the two settings. As we wrote some 20 years ago, "The notion of instructional coordination is not interpreted simply as 'more of the same' " (p. 331). But if it is not just more of the same, then what is coordinated classroom and intervention reading instruction? Let's start by examining why coordinated instruction that is simply more of the same cannot be the answer.

The most obvious examples would be where classroom reading lessons are simply delivered from a grade-level core reading program. If we consider the appropriateness of a second-grade reading lesson for a second-grade struggling reader who reads at the primer level, we can begin to see the problem (same problem with a sixth-grade student reading at the third-grade level). Simply adding more minutes of too-hard reading lessons is an unlikely strategy for accelerating reading growth. The best argument, though still a false argument, I have heard for this design, and yes, such designs do still exist, is that the struggling readers will be required to take the second-grade test (or the sixth-grade test) at the end of the year, so grade-level work has to be offered.

The problem with this analysis is the evidence available. I know of but a single example where such a program produced accelerated growth: the Stahl and Heubach (2005) study of primary-grade reading lessons. In that case, extraordinary effort was involved to make the grade-level curriculum materials accessible to the struggling readers. The five principles that governed this effort were:

- Maintain focus on comprehension even as fluency is emphasized.
- Use shared readings and other strategies to familiarize students with the stories.
- Provide support through many repeated readings of the grade-level texts.
- Engage in daily partner reading as an alternative to round-robin reading.
- Dramatically increase the amount of reading done at school and home.

In this two-year research study, this design was forced on the research team based on a local district decision. Although the results were remarkable, the research team provided much professional development to the teachers and monitored the implementation of the adapted instructional plan. Additionally, because the students were primary-grade readers, the gap between grade level and initial levels of reading was not large.

On the other side of the coin are studies such as that done by O'Connor and colleagues (2002) with intermediate-grade struggling readers. Here, the

Standard versus Responsive Intervention Designs

In the research available there are two broad categories of intervention lessons. The first, and probably most common, is the *standard protocol* design. In these cases every intervention is focused on delivering lessons from a single commercial reading program. These vary substantially in their adaptability to individual instructional needs, with some providing no such opportunities except at the level of text difficulty, and others providing far more adaptability in lesson components.

The second category is *responsive intervention* designs. In these designs the intervention teacher largely elects the instructional materials and the lesson components, and these would vary widely depending on the needs of the particular reader. This doesn't mean that the lessons are not guided by some framework for reading instruction, but rather that the lesson design is highly adaptable.

I find the responsive intervention models superior in the research and in practice. At the very least, in the one study that directly compared the two designs with first-grade struggling readers, no statistically significant differences in reading growth were observed (Mathes et al., 2005). Additionally, it was in studies where standard protocol designs were used in intervention lessons that much treatment failure was observed (Torgeson, 2000).

intervention design varied the difficulty of the instructional materials used in intervention lessons. Some students used grade-level classroom reading materials, and others were provided instruction in materials at their reading level. The outcomes, as measured on standardized reading tests, were striking. The students instructed in materials that matched their reading levels exhibited far better reading growth than the students instructed in grade-level materials. Thus, even when grade-level testing is the measure of progress, providing intervention lessons using materials matched to readers' development produced superior results. The evidence also suggests that when reading-level–matched reading lessons are linked to the grade level classroom lesson content, even larger growth can be expected.

So, if using the classroom materials and teaching the same things as the classroom teacher teaches isn't what is meant by a coordinated intervention, just what is? Consider, for instance, classroom reading instruction that is very narrowly conceived and delivered, say lots of round-robin oral reading and worksheets. This is a case where matching those lessons is a bad idea. Instead, in my view of coordination, you need to keep the broad needs of the struggling reader in mind. When you encounter a struggling reader who is participating in a narrowly conceived and delivered classroom reading program, the first thing on your mind should be breadth and balance. Breadth and balance in the sense of providing, in the above case, much silent reading and discussion of the texts being read and, perhaps, good decoding, fluency, and vocabulary lessons.

However, to even begin to design an intervention reading lesson, you need to know something about the classroom reading curriculum and the lessons your struggling readers will receive there. We call this *shared knowledge* (Allington & Broikou, 1988). Actually, we call having the classroom teacher aware of the intervention lessons, and having the intervention teachers aware of the classroom reading lessons *shared knowledge*. But when intervention teachers at least develop the awareness of the classroom lessons their struggling readers receive, we have begun developing shared knowledge.

All sorts of strategies have been developed to increase shared knowledge exhibited by classroom and intervention teachers (Allington & Shake, 1986). The most effective method I have observed is for the intervention teacher to go to each struggling reader's classroom every day and pick him or her up for the intervention lesson. This means going into each classroom when you pick up the struggling readers and when you return them and settle them in. It might not be obvious, but a person can learn a lot about classroom lessons by just stepping into the classroom for a minute or two every day. Just look around at the work that is being done by the other students and any work left on your struggling readers' desks for them to do. In a very short period of time you will be able to describe differences in classroom reading lessons in your school. You then can use this information in designing the intervention reading lessons.

As for the *breadth* principle, what you will be doing is ensuring that each struggling reader develops that broad array of literacy proficiencies that we see in proficient readers. As for *balance*, by monitoring classroom lessons and designing intervention lessons that balance what the struggling reader engages in and learns, you will be attempting to ensure that struggling readers are not simply developing a narrow set of reading skills and proficiencies (Allington, Broikou, & Jachym, 1990).

A second step in achieving better coordination between the reading lessons that struggling readers participate in is to begin a process that supports the development of shared knowledge about the reading process. There are many ways to accomplish this, but one research-based reform that helps achieve this is developing all teachers' expertise in reading development. Adaptation of any reading lesson based on student performance will require that the teacher has the expertise to note the performance and then plan a useful lesson adaptation. Currently, too many teachers lack this level expertise.

One promising study addresses this issue through developing all teachers' abilities to use the running records assessment procedure to document student reading development and strategy use (Ross, 2004). In this case, teachers in some schools were trained in the running records procedure and in other schools they were not. After the training was completed, student reading development was monitored over time. In the schools where the teachers had learned and were using the running records process, the researcher, after controlling for prior school achievement, found that the running records intervention produced significant improvement in reading achievement.

If you are unfamiliar with the running records procedure, it involves recording the oral reading performances of students. From these records teachers can document strategy use as well as the appropriateness of the text and student reading rate and fluency.

> ### Running records
>
> Peter Johnston (2000) has written a small teaching text that is accompanied by audiotape recordings of students' reading that are designed to foster the skills needed to use running records effectively. The text, *Running Records: A Self-Tutoring Guide,* is published by Stenhouse Publishers (www.stenhouse.com). On the Amazon website the book and tapes currently sell for as little as $25.00 new and $17.00 used.

Improving teachers' expertise about reading development improves the instruction they provide. What Ross (2004) has done is something that should be required of every assessment used in schools: Research evidence shows that using that assessment will improve both teaching and learning. Unfortunately, his is about the only such study available. Providing professional development on common reading assessment tools is important. That's because coordinated reading lessons are more likely when everyone speaks the same language. By that, I mean everyone (psychologists, special education teachers, reading specialists, classroom teachers, administrators, ELL teachers) talks about struggling readers using the same language, the same assessment outcomes, the same curriculum focus. In Ross's study, the language that is used is linked to running records evidence.

For shared knowledge to be a viable idea, all teachers must share some basic ideas about reading development, instruction, and assessment. Otherwise, people are likely to be talking past each other and may not even realize the level of misunderstanding.

One School District's Coordination Plan

The North Warren School District in the mountains of upstate New York spent a decade developing wonderfully coordinated intervention services. This model obviously worked well, since never more than 8 percent of the students have fallen below the cutoff on the state reading assessment since the plan was in place (Walp & Walmsley, 2007). In this school district struggling readers get a daily double dose of reading support from the intervention teacher. The reading specialist works mornings in the classrooms of the two grade levels she is assigned. In the afternoon she pulls struggling readers into her reading room for another 30 minutes of small group intervention lessons. These lessons are linked to the work the students did in the classroom earlier that day. So the lesson might involve reteaching a strategy that the struggling readers did not acquire from the classroom lesson, or, if they acquired the strategy it might involve extended work on using that strategy. Difficult, unfamiliar vocabulary from the classroom might be the focus, or at other times students might simply continue reading the classroom texts and get support for the responses that will be expected the following day in the classroom. The point is that this intervention model provides basically seamless coordinated reading instruction. Struggling readers get both added lessons and opportunities to read and help to maintain their progress in the differentiated classroom reading program.

In the North Warren case, the researcher team and teachers began with but two grade levels in an attempt to improve the quality of intervention lessons and the outcomes for struggling readers. Over a decade, it moved throughout the grade levels and into reforming the classroom reading program. Much work developing teacher expertise about teaching children to read was done, and in the end the school had a remarkably effective reading program—both classroom and intervention. But it was hard work, and it took time. Nonetheless, the reading and writing development of all students was the goal that was achieved.

I will close this section by noting that I have never observed a school where coordination was achieved by mandate or achieved easily. Some schools pose greater difficulties than others, but all can emulate North Warren and the other schools where the reading instruction is seamlessly coordinated and producing real results.

Summary

The vast majority of struggling readers receive reading intervention support that is not linked to their success in the classroom. That is a shame, because the evidence clearly indicates that when reading lessons are well coordinated, far better outcomes for struggling readers are observed. Coordination does not imply that the intervention program would replicate a narrowly defined and delivered classroom reading lesson. Absolutely essential are the breadth and balance principles. But neither breadth nor balance has seemed to be of much concern in the design of intervention efforts to date. That must change.

A few schools have managed to create well-coordinated programs, but it has taken both time and hard work to do so. The question we are left with is whether most schools can create the time and put forward the effort to coordinate classroom and intervention reading lessons. If accelerated reading growth is the goal, they will necessarily have to. As Borman and colleagues (2003) concluded after their analyses of federal data on intervention designs: "Title I students benefit most from having extra time to master the developmental material of the regular classroom" (p. 114).

chapter 7

Delivering Intervention by Expert Teacher

If we want to accelerate struggling readers' reading development, then we must plan our interventions so that teachers who are experts on reading instruction deliver the intervention lessons.

In far too many schools I visit, far too much of the intervention support is provided by paraprofessional staff and inexpert teachers, not by expert teachers of reading. In this chapter I begin with a review of current staffing of intervention programs, then discuss the evidence on the role of expert teachers, and close with suggestions for aligning your intervention staffing with what the research says.

Current Staffing of Interventions

In many, if not most, schools, intervention staff are a polyglot of people. Schools have reading specialists, special education teachers, speech and language specialists, school psychologists, English-as-a-second-language teachers, and, typically, paraprofessionals (variously called teaching assistants, assistant teachers, or teacher aides) and often volunteers, all of whom may be providing intervention services to struggling readers. Basically, these folks fall into one of two groups: noncredentialed or credentialed as teachers.

Non–Teaching-Credentialed Staff

It is unclear, in North America, just what sorts of credentials those staff members who work in schools without teacher credentials might have earned. I say this because staff referred to as "teaching assistants" are not required to be certified teachers in most states, but staff referred to as "assistant teachers" are required to have earned teaching credentials in most states. Paraprofessionals are not required to have earned teaching credentials in any state, but perhaps as many as 20 percent of the current paraprofessional workforce has earned teaching credentials. This situation exists, in large part, because some states currently have an oversupply of credentialed teachers looking for work in schools. In these states, then, some of the paraprofessional staff is licensed to teach.

However, the research on the effects that paraprofessionals have on student achievement is, at best, mixed. For instance, Anderson and Pellicier (1990) found that school districts that had a heavier reliance on aides to deliver Title I instruction were more likely to be lower-achieving school districts. In a statewide study of the impact of paraprofessionals, Gerber, Finn,

Achilles, and Boyd-Zaharias (2001) noted that "the results showed that teacher aides have little, if any, positive effect on students' academic achievement" (p. 123). They noted this finding seemed related to the lower quality of reading instruction provided by aides. Gray, McCoy, Dunbar, Dunn, Mitchell, and Ferguson (2007) examined the effects of aides on student achievement in the primary classes using a matched sample test-retest approach to compare the reading achievement of pupils who did and did not receive reading instructional support from teaching assistants. The study showed that "no added value was found for pupils receiving learning support assistance [from teacher aides]. On the contrary, the results suggest that learning support may have a detrimental impact on lower ability readers" (p. 285).

Likewise, Howes (2003) systematically reviews the research literature on aides in special education. He concludes that an overreliance on aides creates problems when quality of intervention is considered. Evidence available is limited but suggests teacher aides' impact on learning is small, even though teachers are often enthusiastic about aides' presence in their classrooms. Perhaps this is because their presence reduces pressure for teachers to provide more individualized attention to struggling students. Howe also raises the issue of "support," since teacher aides often directed work with little opportunity for students to develop personal sense of responsibility for their work. In other words, he reported that when aides worked with lower-achieving students, they often created a dependency effect—the student came to expect that the teacher aides would prompt them and monitor their completion of their work. Thus, independent work habits were undermined.

Shanahan (1999) argues that sending kids who need expert instruction to work with largely untrained paraprofessionals amounts to "a national bait-and-switch trick" (p. 6). In other words, expecting the least well trained adults in the school to provide powerful instruction to the most difficult to teach students simply has little basis in theory or research.

There are fewer studies that detail the precise nature of instruction provided by teacher aides. Still, the research from 24 elementary schools reported by Rowan, Guthrie, Lee, and Guthrie (1986) and the statewide study by Boyd-Zaharias and Pate-Bain (1998) do not indicate that high-quality teaching is a common feature of the reading instruction offered by teacher aides. But why would we expect adults with limited professional training, and therefore limited teaching expertise, to be able to offer high-quality lessons to struggling readers or to anyone else?

Still, teacher aides account for half of all the Title I remedial reading staff, with high-poverty schools more likely to have teacher aides working directly with struggling readers than is the case in lower-poverty schools. In fact, teacher aides in those high-poverty schools spent twice as much time working with children as aides in lower-poverty schools (IRA, 1994). The vast majority (98 percent) of these teacher aides report providing direct instructional support to struggling readers, with almost half reporting they work with no teacher supervision, something required by federal regulations (USDE, 2000).

Similarly, there has been a tremendous growth in the employment of teacher aides in special education programs. According to a decade-old survey of chief state officers completed by the National Resource Center for

The More Things Change the More They Stay the Same

Almost 15 years age we noted that:

> Currently, the design of instructional support programs [Title I remediation, special education, English as a Second Language] for children who have not found learning to read easy is more likely to reflect minimal compliance with federal and state program regulations than to reflect the best evidence on how best to accelerate reading and writing development. (Walmsley & Allington, 1995, p. 22)

Sad to say but this seems as true today as it was almost 15 years ago, It is still far too common to observe six or seven struggling readers completing the same workbook or test-preparation exercises under the supervision of an inexpert paraprofessional than to observe very small group involved in intensive reading intervention lessons taught by a certified reading specialist.

Until instructional support programs begin to better reflect what we know about accelerating the reading development of struggling readers, there is little reason to expect that many struggling readers will ever become achieving readers.

Paraprofessionals in Education (Pickett, 1996), there were then 500,000 paraprofessionals working in U.S. schools, a number that had increased by 100,000 in but five years. With NCLB and IDEA expansion of funding, that number has undoubtedly increased over the past 13 years. Unlike the original conception of paraprofessionals, today these staff are more likely to be involved in providing direct instructional support and less likely to be involved in routine clerical and housekeeping tasks, preparing bulletin boards, duplicating instructional materials, and monitoring playgrounds, study halls, and lunchrooms.

The NCLB Act provides new requirements for teacher aides hired after January 1, 2002. The law says that these paraprofessionals must have:

- Completed two years of study at an institution of higher education;
- Obtained an associate's (or higher) degree; or
- Passed a formal state or local academic assessment, demonstrating knowledge of and the ability to assist in instructing reading, writing, and mathematics.

I know of no research that suggests that teaching assistants that meet these new qualifications do, in fact, produce accelerated reading growth with the students they work with, but even the U.S. Department of Education seems to recognize that too many paraprofessionals are being assigned instructional roles for which they are poorly prepared.

There is also research illustrating that paraprofessionals can be used in ways that enhance student reading achievement. But the most common design involves both substantial professional development and with lessons developed and supervised by reading specialists. And with all of this, the gains are still smaller than the gains produced by certified reading specialists (Brown, Morris, & Fields, 2005; Ehri et al., 2007; Invernezzi, 2001). In their review of tutoring research, Wasik and Slavin (1993) reported effect sizes of between .55 and 2.37 for tutorials using certified teachers and much smaller effect sizes in tutorials using paraprofessionals. Thus, it seems that paraprofessionals can tutor and produce positive effects on the reading achievement of struggling readers, but there is little evidence that they can produce the accelerated gains needed for these students to catch up with their peers in reading.

Reading Specialists

At this time there are roughly 30,000 reading specialists working in U.S. schools. Out of an elementary teacher workforce of 1,000,000 teachers, this seems a very small number. Also worrisome is the finding that only about one-third of these reading specialists have actually earned a graduate degree with a concentration in reading (NCES, 2004). In other words, two of every three reading specialists do not meet the International Reading Association's standards for their position. This is worrisome because of the expertise issue.

Even the federal NCES seems concerned by this, noting, "Although reading specialists tended to have more educational preparation in reading than did other teachers typically engaged in reading instruction, they tended not to have as much educational preparation as other teachers in their main assignments" (p. 3). Oddly, the NCLB Act sets no standards for highly qualified reading specialists. None. The only standard that applies is the same one set for elementary school classroom teachers. I find it odd that nowhere in the federal rules and regulations of the nation's largest program for improving reading instruction and achievement has attention been paid to the qualifications of reading specialists.

Obviously a teacher could become quite expert about teaching struggling readers without having to earn the reading specialist credential as set by the IRA and by many states. Nonetheless the same is true for teaching mathematics or German, and the NCLB law does not allow those alternative paths to count toward being highly qualified. If we are to provide struggling readers with expert reading intervention, then schools must also be worried about the expertise of the teacher who will provide the intervention lessons. My advice would be for schools to work hard to have as many certified reading specialists available as will be needed to provide expert intervention to every struggling reader.

One scholar's view

We want teachers who use their deep knowledge of subject matter along with knowledge of children's histories, routines, and dispositions to create just the right curricular mix for each and all—we want them to use their inquiry skills to alter those approaches when the evidence that passes their eye says they are not working. (Pearson, 2003, p. 15)

Classroom Teachers of Reading

Nye, Konstantopoulos, and Hedges (2004) examined the effects teachers have on student reading achievement in a large randomized field trial design. They found that the impact of the teacher was the single-most powerful variable in explaining student reading achievement:

> The finding that teacher effects are larger than school effects has interesting implications for improving student achievement. Many policies attempt to improve achievement by substituting one school for another (e.g., school choice) or changing the schools themselves (e.g., whole school reform). . . . If teacher effects are larger than school effects, then policies focusing on teacher effects as a larger source of variation may be more promising than policies focusing on school effects. (p. 254)

In other words, schools might work harder at developing the expertise of classroom teachers and spend less time and money deciding what commercial products to buy. As noted by the federal What Works Clearinghouse, there are no core reading programs that have adequate evidence to make any recommendation about their effectiveness. The same is largely true of the supplemental reading programs that are often used in reading intervention efforts (go to Chapter 10 or www.whatworks.ed.gov to review their findings). Although a small number of supplemental programs have been shown to improve word reading accuracy, virtually none has research showing that they improve general reading achievement as typically assessed in schools. Only Reading Recovery, which is not so much a commercial product but rather an intensive professional development program, was found to have strong evidence of effectiveness in raising first-grade struggling readers' general reading achievement (as well as word reading).

Research, though, will not provide much support for school personnel looking for research-based advice. As Anders, Hoffman, and Duffy (2000, p. 724) noted in their review, the research on preservice teacher reading education represents "less than 1% of the total studies conducted in reading over the past 30 years." With figures so small, they concluded, "We have much to say, but few of our claims stand on solid research base rather as practice informed by practice" (p. 727). Because of this lack of research, the IRA funded a longitudinal study of the effective preparation of teachers of reading. What was unique about this study was that the researchers followed these new teachers from their college experiences into their elementary classrooms during their first years of teaching.

Hoffman and colleagues (2003) report on the major findings of this study and include the following:

- The average number of semester course hours in reading completed by the effective teachers was greater than 6 (students completed more than two reading courses).

- Undergraduate reading specializations were available in over 40 percent of the programs, with an average of 16+ semester hours of reading coursework required in these programs.

- Descriptions of course textbooks and course topics suggested that a comprehensive and balanced approach to teaching reading was represented in most programs.

- Extensive field experiences in teaching reading prior to student teaching were commonplace.

- These effective classroom teachers of reading produced reading growth that exceeded the growth produced by experienced teachers in their schools.

This impressive study found that many colleges of education not only know how to produce effective teachers of reading but they have also designed teacher education programs that accomplish just that. The teachers graduating from such programs were more successful in raising the reading levels of lower-achieving readers because they could do each one of the things researchers have identified that effective teachers can do. Berliner (1986), Pressley (2002), and Allington and Johnston (2002) all found that effective teachers connect lessons to student experiences, foster motivation for learning specific content, help students work toward more complicated understandings, diagnose difficulties in learning, and provide a wide array of learning opportunities matched to students needs and interests.

So one question that schools need to consider is whether they have in place processes that ensure they are hiring the most effective teachers of reading available to them. Because intervention must be all day long, hiring effective classroom teachers of reading is one critical but often overlooked aspect of effective intervention design.

The second factor is the availability of high-quality professional development in reading instruction for all teachers. Unfortunately, most school districts have no such thing available. The best most teachers can hope for is a small amount of training in the use of a new commercial reading product, and even that is not regularly available in most schools. In a large-scale survey of teachers, Birman and colleagues (2000) reported that 80 percent of the professional development experiences of teachers involved the lecture format with only 20 percent reporting a collective participation with staff from their building. They also found that two-thirds of all professional development did not build on earlier sessions. This is not a good report on developing the expertise of teachers.

A few states, actually a very few, have structured extensive professional development in teaching reading for all teachers as part of a statewide initiative. Additionally, a few schools have required all classroom teachers to earn the reading specialist credential in order to continue working in that school. But in large part these are atypical examples, though in both cases they represent the possibilities that do exist.

Why Do More Expert Teachers Produce Better Results?

Think of the answer to the question above this way: Would you be surprised if an expert auto mechanic did a better job fixing your car than you could? Could an expert oral surgeon do a better job removing one of your teeth than you could? My point is that expertise is important to performance in virtually all jobs except those that advertise for "unskilled" persons. There is a reason we seek out experts to solve problems in our lives. That is because expertise is important, actually critical, to high levels of success.

Teaching expertise and especially expertise in teaching reading is also critical to student success, especially those students who are struggling readers. It isn't that less-than-expert adults cannot help struggling readers, they can. However, there seems to be little, if any, evidence in the research literature that indicates that inexpert adults can work with struggling readers and accelerate their reading growth. Instead, the intervention research indicates that studies where struggling readers' growth was accelerated used certified teachers, often reading specialists or special education teachers, to deliver the intervention lessons. In those studies where teacher aides provided the intervention support, students often made reading progress, just not very much progress, toward catching up with their peers.

We have evidence on outcomes of interventions using teachers as compared to teacher aides providing the reading lesson, but we have little research that tells us precisely what it is that the more expert teachers actually do differently than the teacher aides. What we do know from the study by Ehri and colleagues (2007) is that teachers were far better at matching struggling readers with appropriate texts to read than were the teacher aides. They noted that providing lots of opportunities for struggling readers to read texts with high accuracy (99 percent accuracy) explained almost all of the success the teachers had in producing accelerated growth. As for how this happened, they suggest, "Higher levels [of accuracy] may have been achieved either by the tutors selecting easier texts or by tutors previewing and coaching students more effectively through the texts during previous sessions when the books were introduced" (p. 440). It seems to me that teachers should be more expert on both of these possibilities. Teachers should know more about text difficulty levels and about student reading levels than teacher aides should. They should know more about introducing a text effectively and more about guiding students through a text than teacher aides should. This is one of the reasons that federal guidelines call for all lessons delivered by teacher aides to be prepared and monitored by teachers. It is the reason why so many volunteer programs use reading specialists to select the texts each student tutored by a volunteer will read. There are also reasons why reading specialists are typically also asked to provide the volunteer tutors with lists of words to introduce and questions to ask after reading.

When the adult providing the intervention lessons is more expert about teaching struggling readers, there is less reason to use highly scripted commercial instructional programs because the expert adult can create an effective intervention largely on their own. Highly scripted instructional packages cannot attend to learner differences and provide instruction informed by the child's responses. Instead, there is but one script, and thus student responses don't really matter very much. Gerry Duffy (2004) summarizes the issue quite well: "What makes scripts less effective than good teachers is that good teachers do what scripts cannot do—they take charge of professional knowledge, manipulate it, and adapt it to changing instructional situations" (p. 11).

Good teaching, effective teaching, is adaptive teaching. It is adapting the standard lesson in ways that make it fit the reader (or readers) in front of you. Adaptive teaching, then, requires that teachers are paying close attention to what their pupils do and say as they move through the reading lesson. No two lessons are really ever exactly alike because students differ, and even groups of students differ, from each other. These differences may require something as simple as an added example or as complex as reteaching the skill or strategy using a completely different method. It is this sort complexity that makes teaching fun and makes it challenging.

One of the key features of the best teachers we studied was the size of their instructional toolbox. When a lesson, or a set of lessons, wasn't producing the targeted learning, these teachers would figuratively reach back into their toolbox and pull out a different way to teach decoding or summarizing or self-monitoring. The less effective teachers we studied seemed unable to do that. Their instructional toolbox was the teacher's manual, and they had no other tools to reach back and try in order to get the lesson to work (Allington, 2002c; Allington & Johnston, 2002; Pressley et al., 2001).

What we found was that effective teachers of reading engaged their students in much more reading and writing activity than did typical teachers, which meant that they ensured students had easy access to a variety of texts they could actually read accurately, fluently, and with understanding. These teachers were far more likely to model the strategies they were teaching and to foster discussions about what students were reading. The effective teachers were far more likely to limit their students' work in low-level materials such as test-preparation packages and workbooks. And, finally, they were more likely to give students more opportunities to choose the texts they read and the topics they wrote about. Each of these features commonly observed in

Resources

These books will enhance teacher expertise about learning and teaching to read:

Allington, R. L. (2006). *What really matters for struggling readers: Designing research-based programs* (2nd ed.). Boston: Allyn & Bacon.

Cunningham, P. M., & Allington, R. L. (2007). *Classrooms that work: They can all read and write* (3rd ed.). Boston: Allyn & Bacon.

Duffy, G. G. (2003). *Explaining reading: A resource for teaching concepts, skills, and strategies.* New York: Guilford.

Duke, N. K., & Bennett-Armistead, S. (2003). *Reading and writing informational text in the primary grades.* New York: Scholastic.

Keene, E. L., & Zimmerman, S. (2007). *Mosaic of thought: Teaching comprehension in a reader's workshop.* Portsmouth, NH: Heinemann.

McGill-Franzen, A. (2006). *Kindergarten literacy.* New York: Scholastic.

Pressley, M. (2006). *Reading instruction that works: The case for balanced teaching* (3rd ed.). New York: Guilford.

Tovani, C. (2001). *I read it, but I don't get it: Comprehension strategies for adolescent readers.* Portland, ME: Stenhouse.

You can find many more powerful professional texts on **www.teachersread.net**.

highly effective classrooms has additional experimental support as well (c.f., Duffy, 2004; Guthrie & Humenick, 2004).

Our work with effective teachers of reading basically fit well with Duffy's (2004) description:

> The research specified earlier in this chapter establishes that effective reading teachers are not disciples of a particular reading theory, philosophy, method, or set of materials, just as they are not compliant followers of instructional scripts. Rather, they see "the point" of various practices, use judgment to select them when adjustments become necessary, and adaptively apply them rather than faithfully follow certain tenets or procedures regardless of situational conditions. (p. 11)

In other words, these teachers were expert, and because of that, their instruction was flexibly adapted to the needs of their students. As Knapp (1995) noted after his study of teaching in high-poverty schools, "The choice of textbooks by school or district does little by itself to make up for teachers' lack of experience with the approach contained in the textbook" (p. 174). Expertise matters.

Cumulative Effects of Effective Teachers

Most students experience at least one truly effective teacher during the elementary school years and again during middle school and high school. But there is a tremendous advantage to having many consecutive effective teachers across the grades. As Bembry, Jordan, Gomez, Anderson, and Mendro (1998) noted in their study of more and less effective teachers, "There is a false sense of confidence among principals. . . . They assume that if a child is put with a poor teacher that putting them with a good teacher the next year will make up the difference. In light of these data, this is a false hope" (p.16). They drew this conclusion based on an analysis of 3 years' data on reading achievement across the school district. In this case every teacher was rated on the reading achievement gains of the students in their classrooms over this time period. Every district elementary teacher was then assigned a number that reflected which quintile their student achievement gain scores fell into. Teachers who had student reading achievement scores among the top 20

► Figure 7.1 **Differences in student reading achievement with teachers who have produced differing levels of reading achievement gains**

A student has teachers from these different levels of reading gains over a three-year period:

1-2-1 compared to 5-4-4	Latter students' reading achievement is 41 percentile ranks higher (e.g., a 70th percentile reading score vs. a 29th)
1-4-1 compared to 4-1-4	Latter students' reading achievement is 21 percentile ranks higher (e.g., a 50th percentile rank vs. a 29th)

The basic rule researchers found was that the greater number of more highly effective teachers a student had, the higher that student's reading achievement was. Teachers matter a lot when it comes to developing students' reading proficiencies. In addition, the researchers found that when students experienced a truly ineffective teacher of reading, even if just for one year, there was a substantial drop in their later reading achievement.

percent of district teachers were assigned a 5 and those in the lowest 20 percent were assigned a 1. All other teachers were then assigned a 2, 3, or 4, depending on where their student test scores fell. Figure 7.1 shows several comparisons of students' achievement when they had teachers of different levels of gain in student reading achievement.

This line of research was originally developed by William Sanders (1998) of the University of Tennessee. In an article summarizing the key findings of his studies of teachers across Tennessee, he noted:

> The effects of teachers appeared to be cumulative. At the extreme, a high-high-high sequence resulted in more than a 50 percentile point higher score in 5th-grade math achievement than the low-low-low sequence. . . . As the level of teacher effectiveness increased, students of lower achievement were the first to benefit, and only teachers of the highest effectiveness generally were effective with all students. (p. 109)

This method of analyzing student learning is now so well accepted that the federal government has approved its use as one alternative way to examine adequate yearly progress of students. There are several other findings that seem important from this line of research:

- Effective teachers are effective wherever they teach. In other words, when an effective teacher moves from a low-poverty suburban school to a high-poverty urban school, she or he is just as effective at producing reading growth. Likewise when a teacher who is ineffective in a high-poverty school moves to a suburban school, she or he is just as ineffective.

- Effective teachers seem to improve their performances every year. Less effective teachers achieve best results about 5 years into teaching and do not improve their outcomes after that.

- Effective teachers see themselves responsible for the reading development of every student in their classroom. Less effective teachers see struggling readers as largely someone else's problem (the LD resource teacher, the reading specialist). Perhaps because of this, more effective teachers spend more time working with struggling readers than do less effective teachers and provide more differentiated reading lessons to them also.

I wish we had better evidence on just how we might create a greater number of effective teachers of reading. Although we do know much about these effective teachers and how they teach, we do not actually know much about how these teachers became the teachers they are today.

We do know, however, that providing beginning teachers with expert mentor teachers and with a lot of useful professional development and in-classroom coaching can develop teachers who produce better reading growth than beginning teachers who receive neither (Duffy, 2004). But even this finding is a bit murky because we have other evidence that when teachers participated in a two-year professional development project with in-class coaching, there was little change in their teaching effectiveness or their student reading growth (Foorman, Chen, Carlson, Moats, Francis, & Fletcher, 2003). As Foorman and Moats (2004) concluded, "Attendance in professional development courses did not translate to higher ratings of teacher effectiveness in the classroom" (p. 57). So, just doing *something* is not guaranteed to improve teaching or learning.

What sort of professional development improves teaching and learning? We do not have many answers to this question, but there are suggestions in the research that seem promising:

- Standard treatments for all teachers seem less effective than tailored professional development and coaching.
- Teaching teachers about literacy learning and teaching seems more powerful than training teachers to use products.
- Continuing professional development activities work far better than one-shot workshops.
- Collaborative professional development works better at improving teaching than do "go it alone" sessions.

What we do know about teacher expertise, however, is well summarized by Foorman and Torgeson (2001):

> In summary, effective classroom reading instruction on phonemic awareness, phonemic decoding, fluency in word recognition and text processing, construction of meaning, vocabulary, spelling, and writing can maximize the probability that all but a very small percentage of children can learn to read on grade level. (p. 210)

By most intelligent estimates, roughly 80 percent of all students will not need extra intervention services once classroom instruction is effective and when additional reading support in the classroom is targeted to struggling readers. These estimates also suggest that probably about 20 percent of all students will need additional intervention support but only about 5 percent will need continuing intervention support over the longer term (Bender & Shores, 2007; Fuchs & Fuchs, 2005; Pinnell et al., 1994; Torgeson, 2002b).

Time will tell whether schools can increase the expertise of classroom teachers such that many of today's struggling readers won't need extra intervention. Likewise, time will tell whether schools can implement expert intensive reading interventions that will accelerate the reading development of students who need it. We now have sufficient research studies showing all this can be accomplished, but whether we can translate that research into common practice, only time will tell.

Summary

Cruickshank and Haefele (2001) note that we need to consider that different people hold different ideas about different types of good teachers—for instance, they propose 10 types of good teachers, in not mutually exclusive categories:

- *Expert* teachers have extensive knowledge of teaching and subject matter.
- *Effective* teachers bring about higher student achievement.
- *Analytic* teachers use observational techniques to record how well they meet their instructional intentions.
- *Reflective* teachers examine their teaching to become more thoughtful teachers.
- *Dutiful* teachers perform assigned duties well.
- *Ideal* teachers meet standards set by principals and education professors.
- *Competent* teachers pass tests necessary to be licensed.
- *Satisfying* teachers please students, teachers, parents, colleagues, and supervisors.
- *Diversity-responsive* teachers are sensitive to all students.
- *Respected* teachers demonstrate qualities regarded as virtues.

In my view, effective teachers combine the first four categories into a single teacher. I say this because the effective teachers my colleagues and I studied almost always had these four features (as well as several others). But for me, the bottom line is that effective teachers produce accelerated reading growth among the struggling readers in their classrooms. They do this by providing classroom reading lessons that meet students' needs across the school day in science and social studies, for instance, as well during the reading block. But if they didn't have the second, third, and fourth characteristics, I don't think they could accomplish that. I believe this is also true for effective intervention teachers who provide reading instruction of an expert and intensive kind such that they accelerate student reading growth.

I wish, as a researcher, that we had better information on how to prepare teachers of this sort but it seems obvious that many teachers enter their first teaching job ill prepared to teach reading effectively. A few—only a few—colleges of education offer their students a teacher preparation program that far better prepares them to teach reading well. Likewise, a few school districts have beginning teacher mentoring and professional development programs that develop the expertise on learning to read and teaching children to read of every new teacher—but most do not.

We now know a lot about designing effective classroom and intervention reading programs, but most of what we know is not common practice in most schools. Central to both the classroom and intervention reading programs is expert teachers. So, in designing our efforts, far more attention must be paid to ensuring that every teacher is an expert in reading instruction for struggling readers.

chapter 8

Focusing Instruction on Meta-Cognition and Meaning

Too often we notice the difficulties that struggling readers have when reading too-hard texts and assume it is their lack of good decoding abilities that is their primary problem.

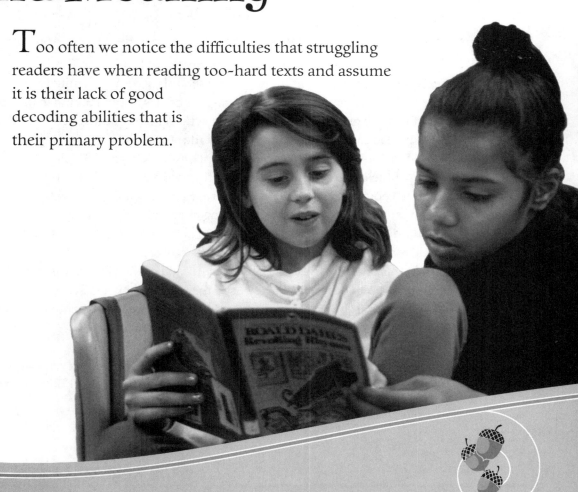

So we provide struggling readers with a decoding emphasis intervention. Then we wonder why they still don't seem to become good readers. The point of this chapter is to help you understand that of all the reading skills and strategies that readers acquire, it is decoding skills that poor readers are most likely to acquire. What struggling readers lag behind in developing is that set of meta-cognitive and text comprehension skills and strategies. Interventions focused on developing meta-cognition and comprehension skills have repeatedly shown to be more likely to accelerate reading development than decoding emphasis interventions.

Why Meta-Cognition and Comprehension Are Important in Intervention Design

A little over a decade ago the U.S. Department of Education funded a large-scale study of teaching in high-poverty schools across the United States. The key question was to identify what sort of classroom reading instruction produced the greatest gains in reading achievement in those schools. Michael Knapp headed a research team that did the study, and their findings are reported in two articles and a book (Knapp, 1995; Knapp & Shields, 1991; Knapp, Shields, & Turnbull, 1992). In this two-year study of 140 classrooms in three geographically distant states, they found that high-poverty schools that offered meaning-emphasis reading lessons fared significantly better on standardized tests of reading and writing achievement than did schools where a skills-emphasis reading framework was in place.

In this study, researchers observed in each of the classrooms as well as collected much other data. They used the Comprehensive Test of Basic Skills (CTBS) as their primary measure of reading achievement. Comparing skills-emphasis and meaning-emphasis classrooms, they found:

- Meaning-emphasis instruction produced reading achievement that was 5.6 NCE (Normal Curve Equivalent) higher on CTBS, which was statistically significant.

- Gains for lower-achieving students were as large or larger than gains for higher-achieving students.

The researchers concluded somewhat pessimistically, "Meaning-oriented practices do not impede the mastery of discrete skills and may facilitate it" (Knapp, 1995, p. 136).

What characterized the meaning-emphasis reading instruction? Knapp and colleagues reported that meaning-emphasis classroom reading lessons:

- Maximized the opportunity to read
- Focused on meaning and means of constructing meaning
- Provided students with opportunities to discuss what was read
- Integrated reading and writing with other subject areas

In the more effective meaning-emphasis classrooms, teachers had students reading much more and for much longer periods of time, and they focused lessons primarily on developing students' understanding of the texts they read. Most striking, perhaps, were the differences in the role that discussion of the texts read played in these classrooms. Discussion was observed in roughly one reading lesson every two weeks in skills-emphasis classrooms as compared to being observed in two-thirds of the reading lessons in meaning-emphasis classrooms. Discussion is one of those classroom activities that has been shown to improve student understanding of what they read, especially students who have difficulty with reading (Langer, 2001).

The final characteristic of the meaning-emphasis classrooms was the integration of reading and writing lessons and activities with other subject areas—intervention all day long. In other words, it wasn't just that the meaning-emphasis teachers had students read and write more during reading block, they also had students reading and writing more in science and social studies as well. They linked the reading and writing activities together and across the school day, not just during the reading and language arts blocks.

Similarly, Puma and colleagues (1997), in analyzing data from national Title I remedial program outcomes, found that the remedial reading specialists who placed a greater emphasis on comprehension and higher-order thinking skills were those who produced higher student academic achievement. They concluded:

> Instructional practices and content emphasis may also distinguish high-performing high-poverty schools. Schools where teachers adopted a balanced view of remedial skills and higher-order thinking had high-performing disadvantaged students. Rather than viewing instruction in basic skills as a prerequisite for higher-order and more challenging materials, teachers in these schools appeared to generally challenge their students with cognitively demanding material. (p. 63)

Unfortunately, there were few of the high-poverty schools in the national sample where this more balanced approach characterized the classroom and remedial instruction.

Given the scope of Knapp's and Puma's studies and their sponsorship by the federal education agency, I assumed that we finally had the evidence that would lead to a push for meaning-emphasis instruction, especially reading instruction, in high-poverty schools. Unfortunately, both studies were largely ignored by the academics and the policy makers who shape federal education policies. Instead, we got a push for decoding-emphasis reading lessons in both classrooms and intervention programs (Rayner, Foorman, Perfetti, Pesetsky, & Seidenberg, 2002).

Research on Comprehension among Struggling Readers

There is little research on the comprehension of children in the initial stages of learning to read. In most cases, research on comprehension includes children in grades 3 and above. There are a number of serious concerns to be addressed in the research about how factors such as limited vocabulary knowledge (e.g., Hart & Risley, 1995; White, Graves, & Slater, 1990), re-stricted knowledge of the world (e.g., Nation, 2005), basic memory processes (Vellutino, 2003), or various instructional methods (e.g., Dahl & Freppon, 1995; McIntyre & Freppon, 1994) impact learning to read and especially how they impact developing readers who understand what they read. Nonetheless, we do know quite a bit about the role and nature of comprehension difficulties in struggling readers (Allington & McGill-Franzen, 2008).

For instance, Buly and Valencia (2002) assessed various reading proficiencies of fourth-graders from a number of elementary schools that had failed the state reading assessment. They assessed each student on a battery of standardized diagnostic tests, then analyzed these data using cluster analysis. What they found may surprise you. For instance, roughly 20 percent of the struggling fourth-graders Buly and Valencia tested were accurate word callers but had little or no understanding of what they read. Another 20 percent had problems with decoding but exhibited few problems with comprehension. They found other clusters of struggling readers who represented slow, steady struggling readers who comprehended well but took a long time to read, others who were deliberate decoders, able to maintain comprehension, and a small cluster (9 percent) of struggling readers with very poor performances on decoding and therefore low performances on every other assessment they administered.

In a similar manner, Leach, Scarborough, and Rescorda (2003) studied the reading skills of fourth- and fifth-grade struggling readers, contrasting their development with that of other students without reading difficulties. Each student was tested on multiple measures to identify reading comprehension and decoding/word recognition development. The tests included the comprehension component of the Peabody Individual Achievement Test, Woodcock-Johnson word reading and word attack subtests, and tests of sight word and nonsense syllable spelling, word and non-word reading speed, and a rapid automized naming measure.

The researchers used a standard score of 90 as cutoff for adequate performance on all measures, and again about 20 percent of the struggling readers exhibited poor decoding/word reading but adequate comprehension, 40 percent demonstrated adequate decoding/word reading skills but failed to meet the comprehension standard, and another 40 percent failed to achieve the cutoff score on measures of either comprehension or decoding/

word reading. In other words, many of the struggling fourth- and fifth-grade readers could not read words accurately but many more could not demonstrate adequate comprehension by meeting the comprehension standard.

Leach and colleagues (2003) also reported that roughly 40 percent of struggling readers had late-emerging reading disabilities—reading difficulties that appeared after an initially successful start. What was perhaps most troubling was that 80 percent of the students exhibiting only reading comprehension problems had not been identified by their schools as struggling readers.

Although this study provides useful insights, the comprehension assessment (PIAT sentence reading task) limits my confidence in the researchers' estimates of comprehension and comprehension difficulties. Had the researchers used more complex comprehension measures, such as those found in any upper-elementary classroom, it is likely they would have found more students exhibiting comprehension difficulties. Or if they had assessed higher-order comprehension—summary, analysis, or synthesis tasks—even more readers would likely have been found to be exhibiting reading comprehension difficulties. Nonetheless, I concur with their conclusion:

> Reading disabilities in children beyond the primary grades appear to be heterogeneous with regard to the nature of their reading skill deficits . . . some children have comprehension problems only, some have just word-level difficulties, and some exhibit across the board weaknesses. . . . Hence both assessment and instruction must be aligned with this reality. Most important, intervention programs need then to be selected on the basis of children's deficit type(s) rather than overall grade level. (Leach et al., 2003, p. 222)

Using a very large sample of fourth-grade children, Rupp and Lesaux (2006) examined the relationship between performance on a Canadian provincial standards-based reading comprehension assessment and student performances on the Stanford Diagnostic Reading Test as well as student performances on several skills measures (e.g., words correct per minute, Wide Range Achievement Test, word identification and word attack subtests on the Woodcock Reading Mastery Tests, one minute pseudo-word reading, pseudo-word spelling, WRAT Spelling, Rosner Auditory Analysis Test, and working memory for words).

Rupp and Lesaux (2006) found that scores on the skills tests did not reliably predict the classification of readers on the standards-based assessment. Although the higher-achieving readers on the standards-based test performed well on the assessments of all skills, student performance in the "below expectations" group was highly variable. They found that 40 percent of these students did very well on both clusters (Word-Level Skills and Working-Memory/Language Skills), 30 percent of students who met the standards-based expectations were low-achievers on both clusters, and 30 percent were mixed achievers (high on one but not the other).

They concluded that their analyses

> indicate that there is an important subgroup of children within the "below expectations" group that has reading difficulties that are not primarily related to component skills of reading. This is a group for whom an intervention that targets foundational word-level and related cognitive and related linguistic skills would not be appropriate, yet these skills are often the target of remedial instruction in fourth grade. (p. 330)

So, we have good evidence that there are many struggling readers with adequately developed decoding skills who still cannot read with understanding. Duke, Pressley, and Hilden (2004) probably offer the best summary in suggesting that there are many poor readers with adequate decoding skills but impaired comprehension, and that the percentage of such cases increases from the primary to the upper elementary grades.

Although there also seems to be a large group of students who lag in the development of both decoding and comprehension proficiencies, it is not clear that focusing on developing the decoding skills will necessarily produce readers who can read with understanding (Swanson, Hoskyn, & Lee, 1999; Torgeson & Hudson, 2006). For some of the struggling readers it may be that resolving the decoding problems will lead to improved comprehension. But the research shows that there will be others, perhaps many others, who develop effective decoding skills and still lag in demonstrating adequate comprehension development.

Here, I agree with Torgeson, Wagner, and Rashotte (1997):

> We still do not have convincing evidence that the relative differences in growth on phonetic reading skills produced by certain instructional approaches led to corresponding advantages in orthographic reading skills and reading comprehension for children with phonologically-based reading disabilities. (p. 230)

In other words, we have both research and a long tradition of providing decoding-emphasis interventions that did not produce students who could read with understanding.

Finally, we have the data provided by German and Newman (2007). They found that none of the remedial readers they tested on silent reading comprehension actually exhibited any reading difficulties. These students were those who had been identified as having "word finding" problems and their oral reading was deficient. But these same students, all enrolled in remedial reading instruction, performed on grade level when asked to read silently and then had their comprehension assessed. This suggests to me that there may be many students currently considered struggling readers but only because we have only assessed oral reading proficiencies.

However, I must close the section by noting that effective decoding skills is one important aspect of reading development. But just as having a large receptive vocabulary is very useful in learning to read and in reading with understanding, having that one component does not ensure that a child will learn to read nor that a child will read with understanding. The same is true with decoding proficiencies. We need to design interventions that include a balanced approach to reading lessons but with an emphasis on developing meta-cognition and comprehension.

What Does Effective Teaching of Meta-Cognition and Comprehension Look Like?

We know quite a lot about developing both meta-cognitive and text comprehension skills and strategies in struggling readers—too much, in fact, to provide anything but an overview here. We will begin that overview by looking at how successful classroom teachers teach.

Duke and Pearson (2002) note that there are several features of good instruction that must be present if we hope to foster comprehension in struggling readers. They cite the following features of instruction that are critical to comprehension development:

- A great deal of time spent reading
- Experience reading real texts for real reasons
- Experience reading a range of text genres that we want students to be able to comprehend
- A setting rich in vocabulary development through reading, experience, and discussions of words and their meanings
- A setting rich in high-quality talk about texts that have been read
- Lots of time spent writing texts for others to read

Their review of the research available then provides further support for several of the other principles for effective intervention design. There is less benefit from useful strategy lessons if struggling readers do not have the opportunity to engage in much reading, especially motivated, engaged reading activity coupled with good instruction and the opportunity to talk about what they've read.

Keene (2002) provides an analysis of exceptional comprehension teachers, drawn from grades 1 through 12, who worked primarily in urban low-income schools. She identified seven common traits of their teaching:

- Take the time to understand their use of strategies while reading.
- Comprehension instruction is incorporated into daily, weekly, and monthly plans and lessons.
- Ask students to apply strategies in a wide variety of texts (genres, topics, levels).
- Vary the size of strategy instructional groups: large groups to introduce a new strategy, or an old strategy with a new genre, and to do a think-aloud to demonstrate proficient use of a strategy; and small groups to provide more intensive instruction for students who need it, to introduce more challenging texts to students who have quickly picked up a

strategy, and to discuss books; and one-to-one conferences to check a student's understanding and application of a strategy, to provide intensive strategy lessons for students who need it, and to push a student to use a specific strategy more deeply.

- Gradually release responsibility for strategy application to students.

- Ask students to demonstrate strategy use in a variety of ways (two-column journals, Venn diagrams, charts, skits, letters to author or characters, sketches, timelines).

- Understand why they teach strategies and how they teach strategy lessons.

Now add to these characteristics engaging students in wide reading and frequent literate conversations about their reading (discussion), and you have a general idea of what needs to be done. (See Keene [2008] for additional information on discussion of books with struggling readers.) Notice I have not mentioned worksheets or skill pages in the description. It isn't that asking students questions after they read or asking them to complete a targeted worksheet should be banned from schools, but, rather, these sorts of activities have been found to be not very useful in developing reading proficiency.

What we have learned is something about the potential power of after-reading discussion for fostering understanding of material read. Applebee, Langer, Nystrand, and Gamoran (2003) studied middle and high school classrooms in five states and found discussion-based instruction more effective at enhancing both reading and writing achievement after controlling for prior achievement and other background variables. Discussion-based instruction was more effective at each grade level and for students from every achievement group and ethnic group. However, they found that lower-track classes had discussions less frequently and of shorter duration (average of 3.7 minutes) than students in high-track classes (average of 14.7 minutes). Even though rare, more frequent and longer discussions in lower-track classes produced higher achievement. It seems that discussion after reading requires students to begin to verbalize their thinking about the text that has been read. When other students talk, they acquire several new understandings almost immediately: that not everyone understood the text the same way and that they are not the only ones who had some difficulty with understanding the text.

> ## Questions that foster discussion
>
> - What were you thinking about right after you finished reading this text?
> - Are there topics you need more information about to better understand this text?
> - Think about the questions you had as you read this text. Tell us about one of those questions.
> - Did this text remind you of other books you've read?

This is the basic problem with questions after reading: If the student cannot answer the questions a teacher asks after reading, what the child needs is good instruction, not red marks on a worksheet. If teachers commonly use question asking or worksheets to help them quickly find the students with problems, and they bring those students together for a targeted reading lesson, then perhaps those activities could be justified. The unfortunate situation in classrooms is that only a very few teachers use questions after reading in this way.

Even in current intervention programs it is unlikely that struggling readers will receive useful and expert reading comprehension strategy lessons. Vaughn, Moody, and Schumm (1998) found little active comprehension teaching in the special education resource room lessons they observed. This finding follows the findings of earlier similar studies (Thurlow et al., 1983; Ysseldyke, Thurlow, Mecklenburg, & Graden, 1984; Zigmond, Vallecorsa, & Leinhardt; 1980). Similar findings have been reported by researchers studying both classroom reading lessons and remedial reading instruction (McGill-Franzen & Allington, 1990; Taylor, Pearson, Peterson, & Rodriguez, 2003). This lack of good strategy teaching is not because we do not know how to teach strategies nor have any evidence of good strategy instruction effects.

For instance, over a decade ago Mastropieri and colleagues (1996) conducted a review of the research on teaching comprehension strategies to students, especially students with reading and learning disabilities. They found that training students to use personal questioning strategies while reading yielded a large overall effect size of 1.33. The key features in all of these studies included teaching students to stop and question themselves before, during, or upon completion of reading to promote understanding of the printed material. Overall, they found a general effect size of .97 for all comprehension strategy instruction provided struggling readers.

In addition, Mastropieri and Scruggs (1997) note that teachers can improve the reading comprehension of pupils identified as learning disabled when they directly teach comprehension strategies that have been identified as effective in fostering comprehension development, provide modeling of those strategies to students, offer guided instruction and practice in using those strategies along with opportunities to practice strategy use in a variety of types of texts, and when they monitor student development and adjust instruction to students needs. However, it is the rare commercial curriculum material that provides sufficient guidance as well as texts to accomplish this sort of instruction. Instead, teachers must typically develop their own comprehension lessons or be able to substantially adapt the lessons in commercial materials in order to foster good comprehension strategy use. This is again where teacher expertise becomes important.

We can summarize, generally, what each of these reviews of the research indicates, by simply reading Duke, Pressley, and Hilden (2004):

> One of the most certain conclusions from the literature on comprehension strategies instruction is that long-term teaching of a small repertoire of strategies, beginning with teacher explanation and modeling with gradual release of responsibility to the student is very effective in promoting students' reading comprehension. This conclusion holds true for students with learning disabilities as well. (p. 512)

However, there are other things that research says about teaching comprehension to struggling readers. Hiebert and Taylor (2000) described key features of reading interventions in the primary grades. These interventions typically were one-to-one or very small (1 to 3 kids) 30-minute intervention lessons. The lessons most often included reading texts of appropriate difficulty along with writing activities integrated with the reading. The interventions varied from one-semester to one-year efforts. The interventions most often used were tradebooks or leveled books, focused on fostering fluency, often through repeated readings. Comprehension activities were common but seemed to have been mostly postreading retellings, summarizing, and discussion. Word study/decoding was also common with word family or word categorization the most common focus. Gains in comprehension were typically reported along with gains in other reading proficiencies. Hiebert and Taylor's review indicates that although these early interventions were not focused solely on improving reading comprehension, improvement in comprehension was common.

> ### Is it our teaching that limits understanding?
>
> Ellin Keene, who coauthored the comprehension strategy text, *Mosaic of Thought* (Keene & Zimmerman, 2007), has a new book titled simply, *To Understand* (2008). In this new book she notes, "I began to realize that the only reason children weren't thinking at consistently high levels was that I hadn't consistently asked and expected them to" (p. 14).
>
> Keene then describes how she now views her use of directions, such as, "See if you can think of a question about the story." She contrasts this with directing students to "think about all the questions you have and then pick one or two that you think will help us understand the story." Providing the latter direction produced far more questions and questions unlike those that teachers usually ask after children have read something.

Other researchers specifically designed interventions to advance the development of reading comprehension among struggling readers. Gersten, Fuchs, Williams, and Baker (2001) reviewed interventions targeting the improvement of comprehension among pupils with learning disabilities and concluded, "Use of story grammar elements to improve comprehension of narrative texts should be considered best practice for students with learning disabilities" (p. 296). They reported that the effective intervention offered struggling readers modeling, demonstration, and guided application of the reading strategies. However, they noted that little of the intervention research included longer-term evidence that pupils with learning disabilities ever developed independent control over strategy use. Most interventions were offered for very limited time periods and included no measure of transfer of the use of the strategies or a finding of no transfer effects. They concluded that the research well supported comprehension strategy instruction for struggling readers but that we still need better studies of the transfer of the taught strategies to general use.

One such study was conducted by Brown, Pressley, Van Meter, and Schuder (1996). Here, the focus was on second-grade struggling readers from 10 classrooms that were closely matched on various characteristics. Half the teachers in this study provided comprehension strategy instruction across the school year; half did not. Students in the comprehension strategy instruction classrooms reported greater awareness of both comprehension and word recognition strategies and performed significantly better on the end-of-year standardized reading achievement test. An effect size of 1.70 on the standardized test score comparison illustrates the power of strategy instruction for struggling readers (Williams, 2002).

Useful Strategies for Struggling Readers' Intervention Lessons

Summarization: Teach struggling readers strategies for summarizing texts of different sorts.

Story grammar/Graphic organizers: Show struggling readers how to use story grammar or other sorts of graphic organizers (e.g., Venn diagram, timeline) to identify important themes in a text.

Question generating/Answering: Develop struggling readers' ability to generate useful and powerful questions as they read a text and how to answer those questions.

Prior knowledge/Prediction: Demonstrate how you activate your background knowledge before you begin reading and how you generate predictions about the text.

Imagery: Visualization is one of those useful strategies we all use when reading. We imagine (visualize) what characters look like and how they are dressed. We create mental images of the settings including the rural environment on the plains where the little house on the prairie stood all those years ago.

What the research says about comprehension proficiencies can be summarized as follows:

- Many struggling readers can decode but do not understand what they read. Others have both decoding difficulties and comprehension difficulties.
- Providing struggling readers with active, expert comprehension strategy instruction improves their understanding.
- Most reading interventions are not now focused on comprehension strategy teaching.
- Most teachers seem to find strategy teaching difficult.
- Expertise is needed to offer effective strategy lessons.

In order to provide struggling readers with powerful comprehension lessons, and we must, teachers will necessarily have to develop proficiency in effective strategy instruction.

This is where the work of Duffy (1993, 2003, 2004) can be helpful. He notes:

In the end, then, helping low achievers become more strategic requires teachers to make subtle instructional adjustments "on the fly," which, in turn, requires different kinds of teacher preparation. Given that most teachers work within the American tradition of following the prescriptions of a commercial program, however, it will not be easy to put teachers in positions where their minds are the most valued educational resource. The need to do so, however, is the most important thing I have learned in this work. (Duffy, 1993, p. 245)

Duffy's research has shown that becoming a good comprehension strategy teacher is hard work that takes teachers a while to master. That does not mean that teacher preparation programs and professional development projects should not take on this challenge, but, rather, that most programs and projects have not allocated sufficient resources to ensure that all teachers become good strategy teachers.

Thus, one aspect of planning a research-based intervention design is to ask the question: How many of our classroom and intervention teachers are experts at good comprehension strategy instruction? If the answer is too few, then providing the sorts of professional development that Duffy's work offers teachers is a good starting point.

Meta-Cognition and Learning to Read

Meta-cognition is basically the ability to monitor what you are doing while you are doing it. When it comes to reading, probably the most important meta-cognitive ability is monitoring whether the text you are reading is making sense as you read it (Pressley, 2002). There are other meta-cognitive strategies good readers have and use, including:

- Knows a number of ways to figure out the pronunciation of unknown words.
- Knows to use background knowledge before, during, and after reading.
- Knows the steps involved in summarizing something he or she has read.
- Knows to construct mental images of settings when he or she is reading.
- Knows when to call up fix-up strategies when the going gets tough.

These are but a few meta-cognitive activities good comprehenders are always using as they read. It is the use of these strategies that leads us to call effective reading, *active, engaged reading.*

Vaughn, Gersten, and Chard (2000) reviewed effective comprehension interventions in two broad categories: comprehension monitoring (using repair strategies) and text structuring (generating questions while reading, using a story map or other text structure guides). I consider both largely meta-cognitive strategy instruction because the students were taught to use a system to actively encourage them to think about what they were reading and the problems and solutions that they might use. Thinking aloud with support of peers is one newer promising approach, according to these researchers.

Vaughn and colleagues (2000) conclude that the evidence indicates that students with learning disabilities can be taught these strategies but that the research typically does not address the issue of transfer to independent use of these strategies. They reported that teacher modeling, scaffolding, and support were essential for successful instruction and that peer tutoring and other opportunities to verbalize thinking seemed central to improvements in higher-order strategy use. They noted that very small group ($n = 3$) instruction led by an expert teacher had the largest impact on improvement of reading achievement.

Walczyk and Griffith-Ross (2007) explain how struggling readers compensate for and overcome various difficulties they encounter as they read (word recognition, syntactic complexity, vocabulary, inferences). They provide a list of meta-cognitive strategies that research has identified as compensations that both developing and struggling readers use when they encounter difficulties while reading. The following strategies are listed from least to most disruptive.

- *Slow down reading:* As reading ability develops, readers gain greater control over the rate at which they read. When students encounter difficulties, effective readers slow down their rate of reading to sort out the problems that the text imposes.

- *Pause while reading:* Effective readers pause when they encounter difficulties reading a text. The pause seems to provide the time needed for an inefficient subprocess to work. Pausing may be the strategy selected when slowing down reading rate fails to resolve the difficulty. It may also be a sign that the reader is working through the confusion or considering other strategy options.

- *Look back:* Looking back happens when a reader briefly glances back at a few words in the text that he or she is reading. This looking back seems to restore information to working memory. Looking back has been documented as useful in determining the meaning of an unknown word or concept, or poorly written text.

- *Read aloud:* Readers will often elect to turn to reading aloud when text is difficult. Reading aloud seems to slow the rate of reading as well as provide auditory feedback to the reader.

- *Sound out words, analogize to a known word, or use contextual guessing:* When effective readers encounter an unfamiliar word (a word not recognized at a glance) they may use any of these strategies to identify the word.

- *Skip a word:* When an unknown word is encountered, an effective reader may decide not to try to figure out the unknown word or he or she works at it and is unsuccessful. In each of these instances the reader may purposely skip the word and continue reading.

- *Reread the text:* When an effective reader finds the text is not making sense, rereading is an often-used strategy to try to get back on track. The reader will reread some of the text, often returning to the beginning of a sentence and starting over, or, at times, reread a full paragraph or more. Rereading a text may resolve problems with syntax, phrasing, and prosody as well as confusions caused by a lack of understanding of what was read.

Walczyk and Griffith-Ross (2007) argue that struggling readers will comprehend text better if they are allowed to, even encouraged to, use any or all of these compensatory strategies. For instance, allowing unrestricted time to read produces an environment where struggling readers can use the slower reading and rereading meta-cognitive strategies. Allowing struggling readers to select some of the texts they read is also important because readers seem to use these strategies only when they are motivated to read for understanding. Likewise, we should work with struggling readers on setting purposes for reading, monitoring their own understanding, and familiarizing them with the preceding seven strategies.

According to Carr, Borkowski, and Maxwell (1991):

Children's successes are dependent, in part, on their beliefs that effort counts and that they are in control of academic progress. There is otherwise little reason to apply strategies to problem-solving tasks and to acquire metacognitive knowledge. If the impetus for achievement is external to children (e.g., a belief in luck or in the necessity of help from others), it is unlikely that they will develop feelings of self-esteem and a repertoire of high-level metacognitive skills (especially executive skills) necessary for good performance. (p. 117)

This is the final aspect of meta-cognition that has been too often overlooked in our work with struggling readers. The term *learned helplessness* has often been used in the research to describe a common characteristic of struggling readers (students who have a reading and/or learning disability). By learned helplessness, the authors usually refer to a struggling reader who is not meta-cognitive and who largely waits for someone to tell him or her what to do or what the answer is. But it also means we created these behaviors.

When we interrupt a struggling reader while reading to correct a misread word or a lack of emphasis, we foster learned helplessness. When we give hints to the correct answer or tell these readers what to do before they begin to read, we foster learned helplessness. In fact, teaching behaviors that foster learned helplessness seem linked to tutorial or very small group instruction (Johnston & Winograd, 1985). Perhaps this is because these close encounters with struggling readers allow us to interfere more often while they read. Perhaps these teacher behaviors stem from wanting too much to help the reader get through the reading. Whatever the source, we must be aware of just how disruptive such help can be in developing engaged and active readers.

Developing independent use of meta-cognitive strategies requires that we model and demonstrate and then leave the reader alone while she or he reads. We might ask the reader about meta-cognitive strategy use after she or he has read. We might once again model just how using the meta-cognitive strategies of simply slowing reading down or rereading a sentence or two might have been helpful had the struggling reader done either. We can create lessons where there is time to preview the text and activate background knowledge, thereby providing a basis for predicting what the text is about. But if we always tell struggling readers to do these things or if we do not provide the time to preview and predict, then it is *us* that is the problem. If we rarely give struggling readers either instruction on selection of appropriate books or opportunities to select what they read, then it is unreasonable to expect that struggling readers will develop any skills in book selection.

Summary

Struggling readers need intervention lessons that focus on developing their meta-cognitive and comprehension skills and strategies. Currently neither seems to be the focus of intervention lessons. But effective teaching of strategies is something that many teachers are either unaware of or unskilled at or both. It may be this problem that we must first address in designing effective full-day interventions.

The research available indicates that meaning-emphasis classroom reading instruction produces significantly better reading achievement than skills-emphasis instruction. The research indicates the same thing about the nature of intervention reading lessons. To date, however, this research seems largely ignored. If we want to design schools such that few students ever struggle with learning to read, much more attention will have to be paid to the research.

chapter 9
Using Texts That Are Interesting to Students

As we've moved through the several research-based design features of effective reading interventions you have probably begun to understand why using texts that are interesting to students is one of those features.

Nonetheless, in this chapter you will find the research base for this feature. You will also find resources that will assist you in finding those texts—interesting and appropriate texts for struggling readers.

What Research Says about Texts Interesting to Students

Perhaps the most powerful research supporting the use of texts interesting to students and allowing students to choose what they read comes from the meta-analysis that Guthrie and Humenick (2004) conducted using some 22 experimental or quasi-experimental studies of classroom reform. What they found was striking. When classrooms provided students with easy access to a wide range of interesting texts, the effects on comprehension and motivation to read were enormous. They report that easy access to interesting books produced effect sizes of 1.6 for reading comprehension and 1.5 for reading motivation. They also calculated the effect sizes for allowing students to choose, at least some of the time, the books that they would read. Here, they found an effect size of 1.2 for comprehension and .95 on motivation for reading. Now remember that an effect size of 1.0 moves achievement from the 16th to the 50th percentile rank! In other words, no other features of classroom instruction were as powerful in improving both reading comprehension and motivation.

Likewise, Pressley and colleagues (2003) observed in more and less effective primary-grade classrooms. They used items from the research-based checklist (see Figure 9.1) that Pressley developed to compare these two sets of classrooms on motivating factors for reading. There were striking differences between the two sets of classrooms. The effective teachers all had far more items about their classroom and their lessons that supported reading motivation than undermined it. For instance, one teacher had 63 supporting motivation items as compared to 9 undermining items checked by the observers. Another effective teacher had 74 items marked by observers that supported motivation for reading with only 5 items marked that undermined motivation. One of the less effective teachers, on the other hand, had 20 supporting and 28 undermining items marked by the observers. Another less effective teacher had 21 supporting and 42 undermining items marked during her

► Figure 9.1 **Classroom factors that increase or undermine motivation to read**

Some Research-Based Motivating Factors Observed in Effective Teachers' Classrooms

The classroom is filled with books at different levels.

The teacher introduces new books and displays them in the classroom.

Students are given choices in completion of their work.

The teacher engages students in authentic reading and writing tasks.

The teacher consistently compliments/encourages student effort, behavior, and helpfulness.

Lessons promote higher-order thinking.

The teacher makes connections across lessons, subjects, days, and weeks.

The teacher does expressive read-alouds.

The teacher emphasizes effort in doing best work.

The teacher uses small groups for instruction.

The teacher models and assists students when presenting new material.

The teacher provides many opportunistic mini-lessons.

Transitions between lessons occur smoothly and quickly.

Classroom management is focused on positive, constructive, and encouraging techniques.

Some Research-Based Elements Observed That Undermine Motivation

Emphasis is on correct answers rather than learning from mistakes.

Frequent reminders are made to students that they will be taking standardized tests.

The teacher gives very little praise to students.

Evaluative information is often negative, focused on differences between students.

The teacher calls out grades or posts grades or papers with grades.

Students do not have choices; everyone does the same work.

The teacher rarely has students working together on assignments.

The teacher is more a lecturer than a discussion leader.

The teacher does not model thinking process for students.

The teacher uses time-outs or segregation of students as punishment.

The teacher provides extrinsic rewards (e.g., stickers).

Extra schoolwork is assigned as punishment.

Activities assigned are routine, boring, and low level.

Lessons are not connected to each other.

Source: Adapted from Pressley and colleagues (2003, pp. 40–48).

classroom observations. These classroom observations well documented that in the same building there are often teachers at the same grade level who create very different sorts of classroom environments for learning to read.

It is classroom teachers who create avid readers. In our work we found teachers in the same building and at the same grade level who differed in the same way that Pressley's teachers did. Guess which teachers had virtually every student voluntarily reading at home just about every night? Which teacher had few students who read voluntarily? As you might imagine, creating a motivating classroom environment and providing students with easy access to books they not only could read but books they wanted to read was the winning solution. But when we design intervention programs, we have good research that says these factors are also critical.

Take, for instance, the work of Rosalie Fink (1998, 2006), who has spent more than a decade studying successful adults who struggled to learn to read. Her analyses of these struggling readers' growth led her to develop the interest-based intervention model. That model includes the following factors:

- Help students find the passionate interest that will sustain independent reading.
- Then provide them with lots of reading on their passionate topic.
- Support them as they develop deep schema knowledge about that topic.
- Teach them powerful strategies as they read those interesting texts.
- Provide mentoring support in helping them find and read the books that will turn them into achieving readers.

This is the model that Fink derived from her studies of these successful adults who struggled as beginning readers. As a group, most did not develop as readers until they were between the ages of 10 and 14, several years later than their typical classmates. But someone—a teacher, a parent, a mentor—helped them find their interests and then helped them find and read books on those topics, which ranged widely from automobile repair, to airplanes, to the Civil War, to snakes. Notice how these topics are basically the sorts of things you would read informational books for the purpose of gathering information. But given how rare it is to find any substantial supply of informational texts in elementary classrooms, many of these struggling readers would have been stuck were it not for the adults who helped them find the books they wanted to read.

These adults read themselves into becoming readers. Typically, however, they read books or magazines only on a narrow topic for more than a year. Then the topic broadened, often getting more specific. But the number of texts these students had read on that one single subject provided them with deep content knowledge about the topic and that worked to help them read the next book on the topic. They developed a supply of at-a-glance words related to the topic, and that also helped them read the next text on the subject. Unfortunately, we rarely observe struggling readers reading deeply on a topic but that is the method that supported the development of reading proficiencies in these struggling readers. When Fink tested them, their tested reading ability was typically at the college graduate reading level. The one problem, however, that was common, was that many read more slowly than typical college graduates.

I'm going to close this section with a reminder that none of us read much of anything that we don't find interesting. Imagine the scene at an airport magazine and bookstand if a traveler rushed up and simply put some money on the counter and said. "Get me a book." If you were the clerk, what would you do? Ask, "What kind of book?" And what would you think if the response was, "I don't care, just a book, any book will do." My point is that when readers do read, they usually read things they are interested in and often expert on. I read lots of Civil War books, an extension of being an American history major in college. I don't read books on the Crimean War or the French Revolution. I cannot explain why but those topics are not of much interest to me.

What students say about interests

One high school student noted:

> In history the first day my teacher passed out a paper with a couple of questions about how you learn, like: What type of issues do you have with history, do you like it? That was the first time a teacher seemed to actually care about how students learn. It made me think about how I learn—I never thought about it before because I'd never been asked.
> (Cushman, 2003, p. 5)

If we want struggling readers to make accelerated growth in reading, they have to read. What better way to foster that reading than to surround the struggling reader with lots of books on a topic he or she is interested in and maybe even has some expertise with? But we have rarely done this. And many struggling readers never did end their struggles.

Choice of Texts to Read

In addition to creating classroom and intervention environments where struggling readers have easy access to a range of text on a range of topics, it is also important that we allow struggling readers to primarily read books that they have selected far more often than typically has been the case (Gaskins, 2008; Guthrie & Humenick, 2004; Schraw, Flowerday, & Reisletter, 1998). Other research has shown that giving students choices, "even when seemingly trivial and instructionally irrelevant, seems to enhance interest" (Hidi & Harackiewicz, 2000, p. 154). Too often in schools today it is the struggling readers who have the fewest opportunities to choose what they will read.

You could take a look at how many books you currently have available in your classroom from which students may select. In an ideal world, that number would be substantial, maybe 1,000 titles. The typical classroom library has fewer than one-third that number, and too many classrooms, especially in high-poverty schools, have fewer than 100 titles available. But the situation is often even worse for the struggling readers. That is because almost all the books available in a fourth-grade classroom are written at a fourth- to sixth-grade level. So now, count the numbers of titles you have available in your classroom collection that your very worst reader can actually read accurately, fluently, and with good comprehension. If you are a struggling reader, currently reading at the second-grade level, you can typically find almost no books in your fourth-grade classroom that you can easily read. In too many cases we only have to look as far as the classroom collection to find out why struggling readers are not reading very much.

We could solve this problem with better and more varied classroom library collections. It isn't that the development of such a collection in every classroom would be inexpensive, but we could buy the books to create wonderful classroom libraries for the same dollars we now use to buy curriculum consumables such as workbooks, worksheets, test preparation materials, and copies of skills sheets and such. In fact, that is precisely how one principal created wonderful classroom libraries in her school, by eliminating the purchase of consumables. Given the research showing that most time spent working with such consumables is largely nonproductive when it comes to reading achievement, it is surprising that more principals have not yet arrived at this same conclusion (Leinhardt, Zigmond, & Cooley, 1981).

The research on student choice is powerful testimony to its importance in developing readers. Turner (1995) analyzed classrooms and found that in half of the settings 73 percent of tasks children completed allowed students themselves to select relevant information, or decide how to solve the problem; such tasks invited more meta-cognition and fostered higher-level cognitive processes. In these classrooms Turner observed teachers modeling strategy use, linking reading and writing activities, and students engaged mostly in small group collaborative work and individual conferences with the teacher, and throughout the day there was an emphasis on student responsibility and control coupled with student choice of texts to read and topics to write about. As in the Guthrie and Humenick analysis, Turner found it was this cluster of classroom characteristics that fostered meta-cognition and comprehension development.

The research on engaging students in reading also points to choice and interest as key topics in the design of effective lessons. Hidi and Harackiewicz (2000) noted in their review of the research, for instance, "Investigations focusing on individual interest have shown that children as well as adults who are interested in particular activities or topics pay closer attention, persist for longer periods of time, learn more and enjoy their involvement to a greater degree than individuals without such interest" (p. 153). In other words, reading texts that have been self-selected, texts of interest to the student, might be just the key for undermining all those struggling reader behaviors (inattention, little reading stamina, limited learning, and a lack of enjoyment) that have been so characteristic of struggling readers.

Choice is not, however, free choice. We might gather a collection of five or six appropriate books on a topic of interest to a struggling reader and then

give her or him the opportunity to select which book to begin with. That is quite different from saying, "Just read whatever you'd like." We could also organize the books in an order we would suggest they be read and tell the student that while at the same time saying, "I may not have gotten the order quite right, take a look." As long as the student has five or six books to choose from, the situation is quite different from the most common situation where the struggling reader has no choices (except perhaps not to bother reading).

We can also work in ways that ease students into making choices across a lesson or a series of lessons. Initially, we might have the small group of struggling readers decide which book to read as a group. Perhaps we will allow students to choose which character they will portray in a reader's theater sketch.

▶ When you allow students to select books they find interesting, you will observe an increase in engaged reading.

Maybe we will ask them to create two questions for students to answer after reading the book, or after reading a chapter. We might allow the student to select which 3 to 5 questions they would include to ask anyone who had read the book. Later on, we might display a collection of appropriately difficult books on a topic relevant to the classroom social studies curriculum and ask each student to select a single book to read and report back to the group on its contents. And we could allow them to decide how they will make that report. In other words, I think it is often unreasonable simply to send a struggling reader to the library (or to a book store) with instructions "to go find a book to read." They typically need more support than that, at least initially.

Helping Struggling Readers Learn to Select Books

To make good book choices will require that we teach struggling readers how to choose books. Having experienced a steady diet of lessons where no choice was offered, and having less motivation to read voluntarily, many struggling readers have no real idea about what to look for when making book choices. Only by providing choices can we foster the development of making good book choices.

One of the first things achieving readers do when looking at a book is to ask themselves, "Can I read this?" I recommend the use of the very simple one-finger rule. If there is more than one word on each page that the student cannot pronounce, the book is probably too hard for him or her. I simply ask students to read a few pages and to lift one finger on their hand for every word they cannot pronounce. Compare the number of fingers raised with the number pages read. Decide whether this book is readable for this particular reader.

The second thing good readers do is to ask themselves, "Am I interested in reading this book?" Once the child has decided that he or she can read a book, the next big question to ask is, "Will I read it?" To every reader of this book, there are hundreds of thousands of books available you have never read and never will. My point is that every time we enter a bookstore, we are surrounded by books we will never buy or read. I've read books, such as *Water for Elephants,* that I would never have read had someone not just gushed over the book. Similarly, teachers can create situational interest in a book simply by showing excitement over it, or reading a bit of it, or showing the gorgeous illustrations.

When teachers create instructional settings where struggling readers can easily find that they *can* read, they will usually find books that they *will* read. Teachers, though, can do much more than simply supplying large numbers of appropriate books and allowing students to select which of those books to read.

How to Help Students Find Appropriate Books

Probably the least likely source to buy books for struggling readers are the commercial catalogs that fill your mailbox at school. The limited supply of books available and the cost of the books are the reasons for this judgment. In addition, there is the accessibility problem—you have cover art and someone's very short summary of content. Typically, you do not have a copy of the book or even a sample page to review. So choosing books from catalogs usually means you make a number of choices you wish you hadn't. So if the catalogs are not the best source, then where should educators turn to find the books they need?

Surprisingly, I'll say the "big box" bookstores (Barnes & Noble, Borders, Books-A-Million, etc.). Recently, I passed a three-story Barnes & Noble store where each floor plan looked almost the size of football field. Although the big box stores typically carry music and video as well as books, in every one I've ever visited it was the books that dominated the space. You can find thousands of children's and adolescents' books in these bookstores. And you can pick them up and look through them, even read them if you like—in many cases while drinking a cup of hot coffee you purchased on the premises. The big box bookstores also offer educators a 20 percent discount, and if you are planning to buy lots of books, an even greater discount may be offered. But for me, it is the availability of the books for review that is the real attraction.

My next recommendation is the *Scholastic* book warehouse in your region. Again, you can pick the books up and examine them, and discounts—often deep discounts—are given. The easiest way to locate the nearest warehouse is to ask your *Scholastic* sales representative, or visit their website at www.scholastic.com. One school I've been working with was even offered a limo service to drive the teachers to the *Scholastic* warehouse. Additionally, *Scholastic* often offers 100 books for $99.00 as another method of buying lots of books. But in my view, *Scholastic* is too heavily weighted to novels and has too short a supply of the best informational books available. This is why I put the big box bookstores as my first choice to look for and buy books.

I highly recommend taking struggling readers on a half-day field trip to a big box bookstore. Far too many struggling readers have never seen one, much less been taken to look for books to read. In most cases if you let the store manager know you are coming in with 12 struggling readers and plan to purchase some books that they will choose, you will get support from store personnel with shopping.

Now you will need some money to pay for the books you will buy. That money is available in every school in North America. But the money is often being spent on other things that do not have the power of research behind them—test preparation materials, for instance, or consumable workbooks and worksheets, or commercial computer software or site licenses. There are no schools in North America where books are simply unaffordable.

So, let's assume that you now have an abundant supply of appropriate books in your room (or at least in your building). How do you help struggling readers go through that collection to find one or more books on their favorite topics? The easiest way, of course, would be for you to find a set of books on that topic and just give those books to them. But that doesn't actually develop the ability of locating books a struggling reader might want to read. At least initially, though, I might start that way and locate a couple of books that seem at an appropriate level of complexity on a child's favorite topic. Let him or her choose which book to begin reading. Then, when the student is done reading those two or three books, begin showing how you found them. In other words, start to put the child to work on the searching process.

An often overlooked source of high-interest reading is series books (e.g., *Captain Underpants, Animorphs, Hank the Cow Dog, Little Bill, Junie B. Jones, Goosebumps, Limony Snicket*, etc.). Some series have 10, 20, or more titles in the series and thus provide the opportunity for a lot of reading practice. Series books are popular with kids. They are even listed on the *New York Times* best-sellers' lists. In fact, when a new *Junie B. Jones* title arrives in the bookstore, it will probably make that best-sellers' list. Hardly any children's books, other than new additions to established series, make the list.

These series books are a mainstay of the big box bookstores. They typically display the whole series, and this allows you buy one or two copies of every book in a series for students to read (individually or as partners). *Scholastic* also sells series books and has huge numbers of these books available at their warehouses.

One benefit of series book reading is that reading in a series provides lots of familiarity, and familiarity makes reading easier (McGill-Franzen, 1993). Because most series feature the same cast of characters and settings, continued reading in the series will foster a better understanding of both the characters and the settings. In addition, the reader does not have a wealth of new names and places to try and read and remember.

The problem with series books, though, is that they are almost all fiction and narrative texts. There are informational series books but most of these series are only loosely related sets of books on a science or social studies theme. The really good informational books are an absolute must in every collection. We have found struggling readers love many of the Dorling Kindersley (DK) titles. These smallish books are typically not written the way most informational texts are written because they have so many illustrations and most illustrations have only a paragraph of text under (or around) them. Then there are the books that received the Orbis Pictus Award as truly outstanding informational texts. You can find a list of those titles at www.ala.org.

To help struggling readers find texts they can and will read requires that you know something more about each student's background, hobbies, and interests than is the case when you simply present a standard lesson from a commercial package. There are a variety of ways to gather such information, including just talking with each student about his or her experiences and interests. You might also note the child's clothing and musical interests, for instance. The shirts that students wear may give you insight into favorite sports, sport teams, musicians, cars, and so on. Observe if students read magazines or paperbacks and notice the titles.

Guthrie (2008) notes that many teachers believe that:

- Students come to school either motivated or not.
- Parents are mostly responsible for students' motivation to read.
- Teachers have to teach for achievement; motivating students is a luxury.
- There is usually not much teachers can do to influence motivation anyway.

But Guthrie states that each of these beliefs is contradicted by the research evidence on motivation in schools. In effect, the research shows that teachers are the critical factor in student motivation for reading (and for learning in general). Certain types of teaching will turn off motivated students to reading. Other types of teaching will turn on unmotivated readers to reading. Parents are largely irrelevant in all of this. When students are motivated readers, they not only read much more but they also learn much more when they read. If enhancing reading achievement is your goal, and it is, then creating lessons that motivate reading activity is in your best interest because achievement improves as reading motivation improves.

Fillman and Guthrie (2008) note that researchers have identified several key teacher behaviors that promote motivation and several that undermine it. These factors have been found to motivate reading and learning:

- The teacher relates materials to students' lives.
- The teacher listens to all opinions and voices his or her opinions as well.
- The teacher encourages students to choose what they read (learn), at least most of the time.
- The teacher allows students to finish if they are reading (or writing) something of interest to them.
- The teacher helps students find their own ways of learning to read.

On the other hand, researchers have also documented the unmotivating things teachers do that reduces motivation to read:

- The teacher stops students when they are reading something interesting.
- The teacher tells students exactly what to do all the time.
- The teacher listens only to people who share his or her opinion.
- The teacher makes students read boring books.
- The teacher gives homework that does not help or promote the students' understanding of the lesson or topic.

When you compare these specific instructional factors with the lists of motivating and undermining factors in classrooms and lessons that Pressley and colleagues (2003) provided, it is easy to see what the researchers saw—too many students sitting in classrooms where there are far more factors likely to reduce motivation for reading than in classrooms that will foster a motivation to read. In fact, I would suggest that the general decline in motivation to read that begins to appear around fourth grade may be more related to sitting in classrooms where motivation is undermined than in any explanation related to the students themselves.

Engaged reading

In discussing the analyses of two large national and international sets of data examining the relationship between reading engagement and achievement, Guthrie (2004) concluded, "Based on this massive sample, this finding suggests the stunning conclusion that engaged reading can overcome traditional barriers to reading achievement, including gender, parental education, and income" (p. 5).

Motivation for reading does decline across the school years. Guthrie (2008) reports that 75 percent of fourth-grade students said, "I think reading is interesting." But by eighth grade, 67 percent reported, "I think reading is boring." In just four years the numbers almost reversed themselves! Is that an example of the power of four years spent in classrooms where reading motivation is more likely to be undermined than not? Probably.

What about Extrinsic Motivation?

Many schools use external, or extrinsic, reward systems to encourage students to read more. It was this issue that the National Review Panel examined. As NRP member Tim Shanahan (2002) has written:

> What the panel did study was the efficacy of various procedures and programs used to encourage children to read more. The issue that the NRP studied was not whether independent reading had value, but what school efforts led children to increase their amount of reading. . . .
>
> The conclusion: None of the programs or procedures has proven it effectively gets students to read more and, consequently, to read better. The NRP did not reject the possibility that some procedures might succeed in encouraging reading, and it called for more research on the issue. . . . No matter what the benefits of reading—and they appear extensive—not all plans for encouraging kids to read more are likely to work. Schools should be cautious about adopting such uncharted schemes on a large scale. (p. 38)

In other words, there is too little research available at this time to support any of the various procedures schools have used in their attempts to increase reading volume. In effect, the research is largely silent on how best to motivate students to read more, in the view of the NRP. However, when it comes to offering rewards such as pizza, t-shirts, or stickers when students read voluntarily, research exists but it, too, is less than informative. After reviewing the 10 research studies available, McQuillan (1997) found there were as many studies showing no positive effects on reading volume as there were studies that support rewards (5 versus 5) as a method of increasing reading volume.

However, Gambrell (1996) tested what she called the "rewards proximity hypothesis." She found that when the reward for greater amounts of reading was the opportunity to select a book to keep, there was a positive effect on reading volume when compared to other rewards that were less proximal to

Kid Culture and Books

When you consider the sorts of books that might be attractive to students, you must realize that in most cases there is a substantial age difference between your students and you. Further, if you don't watch the Disney Channel or read a "tween" magazine, then you are actually from a different culture than your students. I've called their culture the "kid culture." In a recent study (McGill-Franzen & Allington, 2008) we were surprised that when we offered free books to minority fourth- and fifth-graders, the most popular titles, by far, were "kid culture" books such as these:

> *Hangin' with Lil' Romeo*
> *Hangin' with Hilary Duff*
> *Pop People: Destiny's Child*
> *Pop People: Lil' Romeo*
> *Meet the Stars of Professional Wrestling*
> *The Adventures of Super Diaper Baby*
> *The Incredible Hulk Book of Strength*
> *How to Draw Spiderman*

These are "kid culture" books because the topics of the books are ever-present in kids' multimedia worlds, a world many adults are not very much aware of, much less actively participating in. Many of these books will not be easy to find in school libraries, or even in the classroom, but these are the books that kids wanted to read (and did read). In most respects, kids' preferences seem to mirror adults' interest in pop culture. Many more adults read *People* magazine that read *Scientific American*. Remember that one huge goal of any intervention is to dramatically increase the volume of free voluntary reading by struggling readers. Providing books (and magazines) that are attractive and interesting to the struggling readers may be just the best way to accomplish that goal.

reading (e.g., stickers). I would suggest that if you plan on rewarding more extensive reading, then plan to have a supply of interesting books that struggling readers can select as their rewards.

Blessing books

Gambrell (1996) discusses how teachers might "bless" books and, by doing so, open up the possibilities of reading for students. This "blessing" involves simply holding the book up in front of students and saying a few words about it. It might also involve reading a bit of the book aloud to students, or simply noting the fantastic illustrations that are available. Blessing a book takes only a few seconds but it helps struggling readers especially find books that they might be interested in. Every teacher, every day, should plan to bless three to five books across the school day.

It is also important to remember that success breeds success. Ensuring that every struggling reader has easy access to *interesting and appropriately difficult* books will go a long way in fostering greater amounts of voluntary reading. It is also important that teachers of struggling readers praise the readers' efforts and strategy use and praise it specifically. The goal here is to help struggling readers overcome their attributions of failure to their own limited intellectual abilities. And poor readers do, too often, attribute their reading struggles as a function of their lack of mental abilities. They could, of course, attribute their problems to poor teaching or just plain old bad luck, but few do. Instead, they begin to think of themselves as "stupid." Because everyone knows that "stupid" people cannot learn very much, such beliefs undermine even further efforts at learning to read or even engaging in reading (Johnston, 2005).

If we can help struggling readers see that with appropriate texts and lots of reading they can improve their reading proficiencies, then we will see them engaging in the work needed to become better readers and in the extensive practice that is required. Nonetheless, easy access to interesting books and the opportunity to choose at least some of the books that will be read accurately, fluently, and with good understanding are absolutely essential building blocks in producing the accelerated reading growth.

Summary

If we plan to design reading interventions that accelerate struggling readers' rate of reading acquisition, then we must make it easy for those students to locate books they will choose to read. The research is quite clear: Easy access to interesting and appropriate books and the option to self-select at least some, if not most, of those books to read, are essential factors in interventions that accelerate development. Fink's (2006) research with successful adult dyslexics offers sound evidence that interest-based models of interventions have been too long ignored.

In most schools some new investments in interesting books will be required. The money for such purchases is already available but often being used to support the purchase of materials that the research simply does not support (e.g., workbooks, test preparation software, skills sheets, etc.). Buying the books you will need should begin with a visit to a big box bookstore, just to see the possibilities. Focus your attention on what the students are interested in, especially if their interests can be related to core curriculum goals and content.

Finally, we must concern ourselves with the classroom environments in which struggling readers spend most of their time. We can create classrooms that foster both motivation for reading and reading comprehension, but usually we don't. More often, we create classrooms, at least for struggling readers, that are more likely to undermine motivation to read and reading comprehension. Your intervention design has to be concerned with every minute struggling readers spend in school. They need full school days of high-quality reading lessons, not just a research-based intervention.

chapter 10

Questions and Answers about Interventions

This chapter offers answers to several questions that I could not find another place in the book to answer.

▶ What about interventions such as Wilson Phonics, Fast Forward, Carbo Reading Styles, or Accelerated Reader?

The main reason I've not written much about commercial programs is that there is almost no evidence to support their use in an intervention design. This is the judgment of the What Works Clearinghouse (WWC), not mine alone. On the next pages you will find two feature boxes that portray the findings of the WWC when it comes to reading programs. The first box features 24 reading programs that the WWC was able to locate some research evidence on program effects. The second box is a listing of over 100 reading programs that the WWC found *no* research evidence was available to support their use.

The reading programs listed in the first box are evaluated using a simple set of signs. What you would look for is a circle with only a plus sign in it under one of the four areas of reading performance. That sign means the WWC found strong evidence of positive effects on the development of the proficiency area (alphabetics, fluency, comprehension, or general reading achievement). You might note right away that no reading program received this highest rating across all four reading proficiency areas. The closest to achieving this was Reading Recovery, which is as much a teacher development program as a commercial package of materials. A rating of positive effects on achievement requires at least two studies and two schools across studies in one domain and a total sample size across studies of at least 350 students or 14 classrooms.

The circle with a plus sign means that the WWC found "strong evidence of a positive effect with no contrary evidence." A plus sign with a question mark means that the WWC found that the research available suggested positive effects but the evidence was not strong. A question mark means that the research pointed to "no evidence of positive effects" on achievement. A minus sign means the research reviewed found strong evidence of negative effect on achievement in that area. A minus sign with a question mark means that some evidence of negative effects were found.

As well illustrated by the WWC analyses, there really is not much evidence that you can buy anything off the shelf and expect to improve reading achievement significantly. The reason for this, I believe, is that "standard protocol" interventions products work only if the teacher is expert enough to be able to adapt and modify the lessons in ways that student responses suggest.

Reading Programs with Some Research Supporting Their Use

The programs listed below were found to have some credible evidence of their effects on reading development. The evidence was not always positive and most was not strong evidence of effectiveness in developing struggling readers' subskills or broad reading abilities. This chart was downloaded from the **www.whatworks.ed.gov** website in January 2008.

Effectiveness Ratings for Beginning Reading Programs in Four Domains

Intervention	Alphabetics	Fluency	Comprehension	General Reading Achievement
Accelerated Reader / Reading Renaissance			+?	+?
Auditory Discrimination in Depth (ADD)® / Lindamood Phonemic Sequencing (LiPS)®	+?		?	
ClassWide Peer Tutoring				+?
Cooperative Integrated Reading and Composition®			?	
Corrective Reading	+?	+?	?	
DaisyQuest	+			
Early Intervention in Reading (EIR)®	+?		+?	
Earobics®	+	?		
Failure Free Reading	?	?	+?	
Fast ForWord®	+		±	
Fluency Formula™		+?	−?	

(continued)

Reading Programs with Some Research Supporting Their Use   (continued)

Intervention	Alphabetics	Fluency	Comprehension	General Reading Achievement
Kaplan SpellRead	+	+?	+?	
Ladders to Literacy for Kindergarten Students	+?	+?	±	
Little Books				+?
Peer-Assisted Learning Strategies (PALS)®	+?	+?	+?	
Read Naturally		?	?	
Read, Write & Type™	+?		?	
Reading Recovery®	+	+?	+?	+
Start Making a Reader Today® (SMART®)	+?	+?	+?	
Stepping Stones to Literacy	+			
Success for All	+?		±	+?
Voyager Universal Literacy System®	+?		−?	
Waterford Early Reading Program™	+?		?	
Wilson Reading System®	+?	?	?	

Alphabetics:
Kaplan SpellRead
Reading Recovery (also General Reading Achievement)
Stepping Stones to Literacy

Daisy Quest
Earobics
Fast ForWord

That may be the primary reason Reading Recovery did so well—it is largely an intervention design that provides high-quality teacher training to those wishing to deliver the Reading Recovery lessons. So Reading Recovery lessons are one-to-one tutorials taught by expert teachers. The students largely select the texts they will read and they spend most of their intervention time actually reading or rereading texts. Thus, by its very design, Reading Recovery scores better on my intervention evaluation rubric than any other intervention model.

I won't argue that the other products have no value. Many of them might provide one or more of your struggling readers with the sorts of lessons they need. But only you can decide that. In doing so you will also need to decide whether the product needs adaptation to include more reading or a greater emphasis on meta-cognition, meaning, and so on. And because so few products have any evidence of their worth in improving general reading achievement, you will need to watch how your struggling readers develop along those lines as well.

▶ **What sort of assessment might be used to monitor progress in an intervention?**

Because of the research showing positive effects on reading achievement when teachers are trained in their use, I recommend the use of either running records or words correct per minute techniques for monitoring student progress. Both techniques provide curriculum-based information on reading accuracy, achievement, and fluency. But both also require substantive teacher training in the use of the techniques, especially in the interpretation of what the data show needs to be done instructionally. If you make the decision to provide the needed training to every teacher in your building, you could begin by getting copies of Johnston's book, *Running Records* (2000), with its audiotapes, or Shinn's book, *Curriculum-Based Assessment: Assessing Special Children* (1992).

Finally, though, you need to be concerned about children's silent reading development. Both running records and words correct per minute techniques use oral reading samples to assess development. Some researchers have estimated that a dependence on only oral reading samples in monitoring reading development will provide false estimates of many students' silent reading

Reading Programs with No Research Supporting Their Use

Each of the intervention programs listed here was reviewed by the What Works Clearinghouse and found to have *no* studies that met their evidence standards. If we comply with federal law, none of these programs would be in use in schools receiving federal monies from NCLB or IDEA. This listing was downloaded from the **www.whatworks.ed.gov** website in January 2008.

Academy of Reading

Alpha-Time

Barton Reading & Spelling System

Benchmark Word Recognition Program

Book Buddies

Breakthrough to Literacy

California Early Literacy Learning (CELL)

Carbo Reading Styles Program

CIERA School Change Project

CompassLearning

Comprehensive Curriculum for Early Student Success

Concept Phonics Fluency Set

Cornerstone Literacy Initiative

Crossties

Davis Learning Strategies® Program

Destination Reading

Direct Instruction/DISTAR

Direct Instruction/Horizons

Direct Instruction/RITE

Direct Instruction/Spelling Mastery

Direct, Intensive, Systematic, Early, and Comprehensive Instruction

Dr. Cupp Readers® & Journal Writers

Edison Schools

Emerging Readers Software

Essential Skills Software

Evidence Based Literacy Instruction

Fast Track Action Reading Program

Frontline Phonics

Fundations

Funnix

Goldman-Lynch Sounds-in-Symbols Development Kit

Hooked on Phonics

HOTS

Huntington Phonics

IntelliTools Reading

Invitations to Literacy

Jostens Integrated Language Arts Basic Learning System

Kindergarten Intervention Program (KIP) Letter People

L. A. P., A Sound Approach to Pre-Reading Skills

Leap into Phonics

LeapFrog SchoolHouse

Letterland

LinguiSystems

Literacy Collaborative

Literacy First

Merit Reading Software Program

My Reading Coach

New American Schools

New Century Integrated Instructional System

New Heights

Pacemaker

Peabody Language Development Kits

Project Read

QuickReads

Read Well

Reading Intervention for Early Success

Reading Theater

Reading Upgrade

Right Start to Reading

Road to the Code

Saxon Phonics

SkillsTutor

Soar to Success

Sonday System

Sound Partners

Sound Reading

Sounds Abound

Sounds and Symbols Early Reading Program

S. P. I. R. E.

Starfall

STEPS (Sequential Teaching of Explicit Phonics and Spelling)

Story Comprehension to Go

SuccessMaker Reading

Sullivan Program

Voices Reading

VoWac (Vowel Oriented Word Attack Course)

Wiggleworks

WORKSHOP WAY—Instant Personality Phonics Activities

Wright Group's Intervention Program

performance. Some students read aloud well and poorly silently, especially if comprehension is the intended outcome. Many struggling readers read aloud poorly compared to their silent reading performances (German & Newman, 2007).

So, do not rely solely on assessments that monitor only oral reading proficiencies. Instead, use curriculum-based comprehension assessment techniques such as retelling, summarizing, discussing, or even simply answering questions after silent reading to evaluate reading comprehension. You can find good information on how to construct reliable assessments of comprehension in Caldwell's recent *Reading Assessment: A Primer for Teachers and Coaches* (2008) or Afflerbach's *Understanding and Using Reading Assessment, K–12* (2007).

For both initial screening and annual performance reviews you could use one of the informal reading inventories such as the *Qualitative Reading Inventory 4* (Leslie & Caldwell, 2006) or the *Critical Reading Inventory* (Applegate, Guinn, & Applegate, 2007), both of which have strong options for measuring understanding texts of different levels and types to provide a standardized measure of comprehension growth.

▶ What about computer-based reading intervention services?

There are a number of computer-based options that schools are offered, often aggressively, as an intervention program for struggling readers. You may have noticed on pages 163–164 one or more computer-based (or web-based) intervention programs (e.g., Accelerated Reader, DaisyQuest, Fast ForWord, Waterford Early Reading Program) that the WWC found some research support for. But only two, DaisyQuest and Fast ForWord, have strong evidence for their effects, and those effects were only in the area of phonological awareness. However, I would note that Fast ForWord was submitted as a K–1 program, and so two studies, both using slightly older students, were excluded from the analysis. In these two studies, Fast ForWord was found ineffective in improving alphabetics skills and all other measured skills (Pokorni, Worthington & Jamison, 2004; Rouse & Krueger, 2004).

Pokorni and colleagues (2004) compared the effects of three beginning reader programs (Fast ForWord, Earobics, and LIPs) on the development of phonemic awareness skills. The struggling readers were aged 7.5 to 9.0 years old and received 60 hours of instruction in each program. The researchers found no gains associated with the use of Fast ForWord. The other two programs did improve phonemic awareness but produced no improvements on any of the reading skills assessments. Rouse and Krueger (2004) randomly assigned over 500 third- through sixth-grade students to participate in a Fast ForWord intervention or not. All of these students fell in the bottom 20 percent of the school district's students based on reading ability. They found no gains were produced by the Fast ForWord intervention that were not also observed in the nonparticipating students. The researchers concluded that there was no benefit in using this program with these students.

Likewise, a few other computer-based programs were awarded the potential evidence ranking by WWC. Even here, though, the evidence base was very slim and the gains quite small. In other words, accelerated reading gains were not observed in these studies. In addition, as Slavin (2007) wrote, the WWC process does emphasize experimental studies but also "the clearinghouse gives its highest ratings for evidence of positive effects to programs supported by studies that are often very small, very brief, very biased, and/or very seriously flawed in other way." He singled out the studies the WWC used to rate DaisyQuest, a computer-based program for developing phonemic awareness for criticism. Slavin also noted that the studies involved only about 5 hours of instruction and the comparison children received no phonemic awareness lessons. Nonetheless, DaisyQuest was found to be more effective than nothing. He also notes another study, one the WWC did not use, and found that a teacher teaching phonemic awareness produced results superior to the DaisyQuest results.

In short, then, the research suggests that most computer-based intervention programs are not very effective at raising reading achievement. I'm not actually surprised by this because so many of the available programs are, literally, worksheets offered via computer. There is a potential for powerful computer-based interventions but such interventions have not yet been developed.

▶ Is Reading Recovery effective?

The review of the research by WWC, O'Connor and Simic (2002), Lyons and Beaver (2007), Schwartz (2005), and D'Agostino and Murphy (2004) demonstrates that Reading Recovery does accelerate reading development of first-grade struggling readers and thereby reduces the numbers of students who are referred to and placed in special education classes. In fact, the evidence supporting Reading Recovery makes the lack of evidence that the WWC was able to locate for other intervention plans an embarrassing situation.

Reading Recovery has grown over the years since its introduction to North America through the Ohio State University, but it remains a largely untapped resource used in only some schools. This may be because of its intense focus on training teachers to deliver the intervention design and its reluctance to endorse any intervention design outside of one-to-one tutoring. Thus, Reading Recovery is an expensive proposition at first glance. I say this because when one calculates the true cost of other options (e.g., special education services or retention in grade), using the Reading Recovery intervention with struggling first-graders is actually less expensive and it enjoys a level of success seldom observed in school intervention designs.

The good news is that we know more about how to design effective intervention lessons that accelerate reading development than we ever have. I use the term *accelerate* purposely because in order to actually solve the problems struggling readers face every day we must catch them up with their achieving classmates and accelerating their reading development is the only solution. So consider Reading Recovery as one potential mode for first-grade struggling readers but use the research to design similarly effective interventions for all the other grades.

▶ What about brain research on struggling readers?

Almost every educator has heard or read something about brain-based teaching. The problem is that no actual research on brain-based teaching exists, and very little research has been done on the function of the brain during reading. We do know that readers' brains seem to work differently than non-readers brains, and that better readers' brains work differently from struggling readers' brains (Shaywitz, 1996). However, notions that struggling readers' brains can be repaired seem more to reflect the fact that teaching struggling readers to read better makes their brains operate more like better readers' brains. This likely means that we have been more successful in teaching reading to these students than any evidence we know about how to repair brain functioning (Coles, 2004).

Goswami (2004) noted what she labeled "neuromyths." She listed several of these that seem commonly believed in too many schools:

- Left-brain/right brain learning/learners
- Critical periods of plasticity for certain sorts of learning
- Male/female brains

She has written that virtually no credible evidence from neuroscience suggests that such things exist, and further, that no evidence exists that any of these three neuromyths have anything to do with achievement gaps that currently exist.

Whenever anyone attempts to convince you about what the research says about brains and learning, I suggest you simply ask for references to at least three full research articles that demonstrate that learning.

▶ What about reading coaches and the RTI effort?

This is a tricky question to answer—tricky because we have only a small bit of research available on reading coaches and their effects on teaching and learning. That said, the coaching model has some, but not much, research that supports its use, and there is very little research on coaches improving literacy teaching or learning.

In addition to the research, I have my own experiences working with schools. I have been appalled that some reading coaches that I have met were folks with no background in reading—former high school journalism teachers, for instance, or former classroom teachers whose only training in reading was a two-day y'all come workshop with hundreds of others. The training too many of these coaches received was shallow and rule bound. Then they were placed in schools to ensure that teachers followed the rules they had been given. Unfortunately, those rules often bore no resemblance to the research on effective teaching.

On the other hand, I have observed other reading coaches with both a reading specialist credential plus good training on how to coach effectively. In these schools, classroom teachers were receiving good advice on improving their reading instruction.

So my answer on reading coaches is: It depends. If you are talking about reading coaches who meet the International Reading Association's criteria for reading coaches and who have participated in good training on how good coaching goes, then I'd probably support their use, even given the lack of good research supporting this model. On the other hand, if the reading coaches do not meet the IRA standards and simply have been trained on a checklist of required classroom instructional factors, then I'd say no, don't use them.

What we do know is that high-quality professional development followed by in-class support (coaching) works to improve teaching and learning over time. Thus, the reading coaches model has, in my eyes, the potential to support classroom teachers as they develop into expert teachers of reading.

resources

Internet resources on reading coaches

www.reading.org/resources/issues/positions_coach.html

www.literacycoachingonline.org/

► You don't really mention dyslexic students in the book. Why is that?

Dyslexia is now one of the federal disability categories that fall under the broader term *Specific Learning Disability (SLD)*. The whole question of whether such things as an SLD exist is being challenged by both researchers and policy makers. These challenges include questions about whether "dyslexia" actually exists. The question is important and, for many folks, emotional.

Since its inception as "word blindness" well over 100 years ago, dyslexia has been attributed primarily to students who had attended school, exhibited typical development in other areas, and yet were unable to read. Over time, the label *dyslexia* became attached to children (and adults) who could read but could not read very well even after instruction. Dyslexia was more recently compared to the label *obese* by noting one could be obese or grossly obese and anywhere in between. Similarly, Shaywitz and colleagues (1992) argued that dyslexics simply were those children who occupied the very lowest end of the normal curve distribution of reading achievement. In other words, children whose reading achievement fell in the first or second percentile ranks might be the dyslexics in a population. This notion seemed to fit the traditional conceptualization of dyslexia as contributing to the reading difficulties of 1 or 2 percent of the total population.

But the original federal law defining SLD limited identification to 2 percent of the population, although that limitation was later eliminated, and now SLD students account for roughly half of all pupils with disabilities. However, that 2 percent theme emerged again under NCLB when schools were allowed to exclude that proportion of kids from annual testing. That percentage was developed using the research showing that 98 percent all students could achieve normal reading levels when provided intensive, expert interventions in kindergarten and grade 1. However, given that some school districts have over one-quarter of the students classified as SLD and some states have roughly one of every five students identified as SLD, there is obviously a huge gap between research, policy, and practice.

In writing this book I typically used the broadest term, *struggling readers,* to describe students who would benefit from intensive, expert reading interventions. I did that largely because there exists no evidence that dyslexic or SLD students benefit from any different form of remediation than all those other unlabeled struggling readers (Allington, 2002; Torgeson & Hudson, 2006; Vellutino & Fletcher, 2005).

So, while there are dyslexia gurus who would argue with me on every point I just made, I will suggest the arguments they offer will come not from research but from ideological positions that research fails to support. Supposed dyslexics seem to be instructionally needy children, most of whom do not receive sufficient expert, intensive reading instruction. I will admit that Fink's (2006) book on successful adult dyslexics suggests that dyslexics may also be children who simply were not ready to learn at age 6 but when provided powerful instruction at ages 10, 12, or 14 they learned to read (Fink's dyslexics read at the college graduate level). Perhaps the reason that less successful dyslexics never learned to read is that no one offered beginning reading instruction to them in middle school.

My closing comment is this: If you have children who have been labeled dyslexic, ignore the label and provide intensive, expert reading instruction for as long as it takes to catch those children up to level.

Appendix A

A Rubric for Evaluating Reading Intervention Designs

5	4	3	2	1
One-to-one tutorials	[Circle in-between columns if your response falls between these provided descriptions.]	Groups of 1 to 3 children		Groups of 4 to 7 children
Pupil/text matches		Most pupil/text matches		Standard texts with little pupil/text matching
Triples daily reading volume		Doubles daily reading volume		No increase in reading volume
Expert teacher provides instruction		Certified teacher provides instruction		Teaching assistant, aide, or volunteer provides instruction
Focused on meaning and meta-cognition development		Some focus on meaning and meta-cognition		Focused on skills development in isolation
Easy access to interesting texts and student choice		Easy access to interesting texts; some student choice		Standard texts with no student choice
Well coordinated with classroom lessons		Some coordination with classroom lessons		Standard texts with no coordination with classroom lessons
Monitoring of student progress is frequent and full—running records, QRI, oral and silent reading comprehension		Monitoring student progress is sporadic but full		Monitoring student progress is narrow—DIBELS or AIMSWeb

Points   5   4   3   2   1

Rating your program's proximity to research-based principles of intervention and then working to improve your rating based on which aspects produce the worst scores will accelerate student reading development.

40 Points	Very well designed	25 points	Not well matched to research
35 points	Well designed	20 points	Close to traditional designs
30 points	Design could be improved	15 points or less	Not a research-based design

Appendix B

Over 100 High-Interest/ Lower-Readability Books for the Middle Grades

Third-Grade Reading Level

Animorphs #1: Invasion by K. A. Applegate

Animorphs #2: Visitor by K. A. Applegate

Assassination of Abraham Lincoln
    by Kay Melchisedech Olson

Battle of the Alamo by Matt Doeden

Blackwater by Eve Bunting

Boy at War by Harry Mazer

Boy No More by Harry Mazer

Bull Rider by Marilyn Halvorson

Burn Out by Paul Kropp

Cliffhanger by Skip Press

Condor Hoax by Elaine Pageler

Cottonmouths by Linda George

Crash by Jerry Spinelli

Danger on Midnight River by Gary Paulsen

Dead On by Paul Kropp

Disappearing Act by Sid Fleischman

Doing Time Online by Jan Siebold

Drive-By by Lynne Ewing

Fast Company by Rich Wallace

Gang War by Paul Kropp

Gold Rush Fever by Penn Mullin

Himalaya by Jonathan Neale

*Ice Mummy: The Discovery of a 5,000-Year-Old
    Man* by Cathy & Mark Dubowski

Iditarod: Story of the Last Great Race
    by Ian Young

Mauna Loa: World's Largest Active Volcano
    by Joanne Mattern

Mean Waters by Frank Woodson

Mountain Blizzard by Ed Hanson

Nightmare Room #1: Don't Forget Me!
    by R. L. Stine

Nightmare Room #3: My Name Is Evil
    by R. L. Stine

Source: Shatmeyer, K. (2007). Hooking struggling readers: Using books they can and want to read. *Illinois Reading Council Journal, 35*(1), 7–13. Used with permission of the Illinois Reading Council.

Pack by Susannah Brin

Rising Water by P. J. Petersen

S.O.R. Losers by Avi

Seikan Railroad Tunnel: World's Longest Tunnel
    by Mark Thomas

Sinking of the Titanic by Matt Doeden

South by Southeast by Anthony Horowitz

Stick Like Glue by Colin Wells

*Storm Chasers: On the Trail of Deadly
    Tornadoes* by Matt White

Tentacles!: Tales of the Giant Squid
    by Shirley Raye Redmond

Then Again, Maybe I Won't by Judy Blume

Treasure Hunting: Looking for Lost Loot
    by Caitlin Scott

Volcano! When a Mountain Explodes
    by Linda Barr

What Do Fish Have to Do With Anything?
    by Avi

White Water by P. J. Petersen

Fourth-Grade Reading Level

Air Disasters by Ann Weil

Amazon Adventure by Ed Hanson

Among the Betrayed by Margaret P. Haddix

Attack Helicopters: The AH-64 Apaches
    by Bill Sweetman

Attack Submarines: The Seawolf Class
    by Michael & Gladys Green

Bear Attacks by Patrick Fitzgerald

Blue Moon by Marilyn Halvorson

BMX Bikes by Kathleen W. Deady

Brickyard 400 by A. R. Schaefer

Buzzard's Feast by Todd Strasser

Call of the Wild—Saddleback Classics
    by Jack London

Camp Wild by Pam Withers

Castles: Towers, Dungeons, Moats, and More
    by Matt White

Choosing Up Sides by John Ritter

Civil War Sub: The Mystery of the Hunley
    by Kate Boehm Jerome

Cobras by Linda George

Countess & Me by Paul Kropp

Danger at 20 Fathoms by Ed Hanson

Deadly Game by Janet Lorimer

Deer Hunting by Randy Frahm

Desert Ordeal by Ed Hanson

Dirt Bike by Paul Kropp

Early Winter by Marion Dane Bauer

Emergency Quarterback: Winning Season
    by Rich Wallace

Escape from Fire Mountain by Gary Paulsen

Escaping the Giant Wave by Peg Kehret

Forged by Fire by Sharon M. Draper

Forming a Band by A. R. Schaefer

Frozen Fire: A Tale of Courage
    by James A. Houston

Gadget by Paul Zindel

Harley-Davidson Motorcycles by Eric Preszler

Heroes Don't Run: A Novel of the Pacific War
    by Harry Mazer

*Hindenburg: The Fiery Crash of a German
    Airship* by Kathleen W. Deady

*History of Skateboarding: From the Backyard to
    the Big Time* by Michael J. Martin

Hostages by Ed Hanson

Hot Cars by Paul Kropp

Into the Dream by William Sleator

*Inventions: Great Ideas and Where They Came
    From* by Sarah Houghton

Jet Fighter Planes by A. R. Schaefer

Lost at Sea by Ed Hanson

Million Dollar Shot by Dan Gutman

Monster Trucks by A. R. Schaefer

*Moon Over Tennessee: A Boy's Civil War
    Journal* by Craig Crist-Evans

Mount St. Helen's Volcano by William Bankier

Night the Heads Came by William Sleator
Party Girl by Lynne Ewing
Pass by Ed Hanson
Return of the Eagle by Paul Buchanan
Rewind by William Sleator
Roar of the Crowd by Rich Wallace
Runt by Marion Dane Bauer
Scott O'Grady: Behind Enemy Lines
    by Barbara A. Somerville
Sea Disasters by Ann Weil
Search and Rescue by Susannah Brin
Shackleton Expedition by Jil Fine
Shark: The Truth Behind the Terror
    by Mike Strong

Shipwreck by Gordon Korman
Skateboarding Greats: Champs of the Ramps
    by Angie Peterson Kaelberer
Skeleton Man by Joseph Bruchac
Skull Talks Back and Other Haunting Tales
    by Zora Neale Hurston & Joyce Thomas
Someone Is Hiding on Alcatraz Island
    by Eve Bunting
Something Upstairs by Avi
Spies! Real People, Real Stories
    by Laura Portalupi
Stealth Bombers by Bill Sweetman
*Sword of the Samurai: Adventure Stories from
    Japan* by Eric A. Kimmel

Book Study Guide

for

What Really Matters in Response to Intervention

Prepared by Lisa Wiedmann,
Former District Director of Reading,
Rhinelander Public Schools, Rhinelander, WI

Book Study Guidelines

Reading, reacting, and interacting with others about a book is one of the ways many of us process new information. Book studies are a common feature in many school districts because they recognize the power of collaborative learning. The intent of a book study is to provide a supportive context for accessing new ideas and affirming best practices already in place. Marching through the questions in a lockstep fashion could result in the mechanical processing of information; it is more beneficial to select specific questions to focus on and give them the attention they deserve.

One possibility to structure your book discussion of *What Really Matters in Response to Intervention* is to use the Reading Reaction Sheet on page 190. Following this format, make a copy for each group member. Next, select a different facilitator for each chapter. The facilitator will act as the official note taker and be responsible for moving the discussion along. He or she begins by explaining that the first question is provided to start the group discussion. The remaining three questions are to be generated by the group. The facilitator can ask each person to identify at least one question and then let the group choose the three they want to cover, or the facilitator can put the participants into three groups, with each group responsible for identifying one question. The three questions are shared for all to hear (and write down), and then discussion of Question 1 commences. The facilitator paces the discussion so the most relevant information for that group is brought out. Since many school districts require documentation for book studies, the facilitator could file the sheet with the appropriate person as well as distribute a copy to all group members for their notes.

Another possibility is to use the guiding questions for each chapter. You could have the same facilitator for all chapters. Perhaps this would be someone who read the book first and suggested it to the group. Or the facilitator role could rotate. It is suggested that the facilitator not only pace the group through the questions to hit on the most important information for the group's needs, but also he or she should take notes for later distribution to group members and/or administrators if required for documentation.

The provided questions are meant to provoke discussion and might lead the group into areas not addressed in the questions. That is wonderful! The importance of a book study is to move the members along in their understanding of the book content. If time is limited, the facilitator might select certain questions from the list for the initial focus of the discussion, allowing other questions as time permits.

Of course, a third option is to combine the two structures. Select the format that best fits your group and the time frame you have set for completion of the book.

All book sessions should end with a purpose for reading the next chapter. It could be to generate questions the group still has, to find implications for each person's own teaching, or to identify new ideas. Purpose setting is a time-honored way to help readers (of any age) approach the text. If you are using the questions that accompany each chapter, direct the participants to read the questions prior to reading the chapter. This will provide a framework for processing the information in the chapter.

Book Study Questions for Each Chapter

chapter 1: Why Struggling Readers Continue to Struggle

1. Allington begins this chapter by stating that "most struggling readers never catch up with their higher-achieving classmates because schools create school days for them where they struggle all day long." Discuss whether most students who receive Title I support in your school ever catch up. Do most students receiving special education support catch up?

2. On a scale from 1 to 5, rate your school, with 1 meaning your school uses only a core text in each subject area and 5 meaning your school has completely adopted a "multitext, multilevel" curriculum design. Explain the reasons for your rating.

3. Do you agree or disagree with Allington's belief that federal funds should be "looked on as a gift to help schools get started" to improve instruction and that local taxpayers should fund the rest? Explain your thoughts.

4. Allington refers to a shift in thinking from what is "wrong" with the student to what needs to be different with the instruction. Where do you think most teachers in your district are in making this shift?

   - I doubt whether any have ever thought of it that way.
   - Some would think like Allington; most wouldn't.
   - We know we have to make the changes and are working toward that end.

5. In your district, where do struggling readers have the most opportunity to receive reading support: K–2, 3–5, 6–8, or 9–12? How and/or why is this so?

6. How many of the schools in your district have a kindergarten intervention program in place? Who provides the intervention instruction for kindergartners who need extra support?

7. Discuss who in your district provides most of the instructional support for struggling readers (certified teachers or noncertified staff). Why is this so?

8. Discuss any innovative options your district has developed to provide intervention instruction for struggling readers without taking time out of the reading block.

9. Given Allington's comments, would you describe your present intervention program as maintaining the development, improving the development, or accelerating the development of struggling readers? Explain your answer.

10. After reading this chapter, why do you believe struggling readers continue to struggle?

11. What information in this chapter will be most helpful to you? Why?

chapter 2: Beginning an Intervention Plan

1. Do you believe that if you looked, you would find that the struggling readers in your district have desks, lockers, and/or backpacks full of books most of which they can actually read with success, a few of which they can actually read with success, or just one book or no books which they can actually read with success?

2. At which grade level would you most likely find specialist teachers using classroom texts during intervention instruction? Why is that?

3. If teachers know that all their students cannot read the science text, social studies text, or class novel, why do you think we still see teachers using the one-size-fits-all text for instruction?

4. Do your intervention specialists use one certain program (commercial or noncommercial) for all struggling readers? Given what Allington says about the varying dimensions of struggling readers, would this be a good plan?

5. Allington talks about all-day-long intervention. What percentage of your teachers, K–2, 3–5, 7–8, or 9–12, use a multilevel, multisource curriculum plan?

6. In your district where are you most likely to see large amounts of whole group instruction: K–2, 3–5, 7–8, or 9–12? Why do you think this is so?

7. Use Allington's reader/text matching tool with students in your classroom/school. What did you learn from the data?

8. How might using the *classroom lessons organization tool* help improve instruction in your school?

9. After reading this chapter, where will you begin your intervention plan?

10. What information in this chapter will be most helpful to you? Why?

chapter 3: Matching Reader and Text Level

1. Allington argues that 99 percent might be an even better accuracy rate for most school reading assignments rather than the more traditional recommendation of 95 percent accuracy. From your experience, which of these makes most sense to you?

2. Think about whether most of the interventions in your school/district are carried out in materials matched to children's reading levels or in materials matched to their current grade placement level. Does the research Allington cites support what is being practiced?

3. Allington describes a study that had success using grade-level materials in interventions. If any of your interventions are using grade-level materials, how similar/different is the design from the one Allington cites?

4. Thinking of your classroom library, how many books do you think you have that your struggling readers can read with 99 percent accuracy, fair to good fluency, and 90 percent comprehension?

5. If you've leveled books in your classroom or library, what formula did you use and how well do you think it worked?

6. Have you developed any strategies of your own to help match students with appropriate texts?

7. After reading this chapter, what will you do to improve the match between reader and text level?

8. What information in this chapter will be most helpful to you? Why?

chapter 4: Dramatically Expand Reading Activity

1. Discuss whether your present intervention design is accelerating the reading growth of your struggling readers at more than one year's growth per year.

2. What might you do to ensure that struggling readers in your intervention programs are engaged in reading high-success texts for Allington's recommended two-thirds of the intervention period?

3. Observe your most struggling readers during an entire reading block. Chart (or have a teacher aide chart) the amount of time each spends actually engaged in reading. Make a chart with the following possible headings. Put a check mark for each student for each minute spent on each activity. Discuss your findings. (Possible headings: Oral Reading, Silent Reading, Looking at Books, Receiving Instruction, Doing Worksheets, Working on a Computer Program, Writing.)

4. Allington mentions the importance of initial success in learning to read. In your experience, when initial instruction wasn't successful, did you see changes in the delivery of instruction or more often changes in something else (i.e., materials, amount of time, etc.)?

5. Use Allington's method to gather number-of-words read data on your struggling readers and discuss the results.

6. Consider Allington's time allotment recommendations for intervention designs. How do your intervention designs compare?

7. Discuss how your school/classroom libraries compare with the standards Allington recommends for access to appropriate texts, including informational texts.

8. Have you discovered ways to fund the purchase of more books that have worked well?

9. After reading this chapter, how do you plan to dramatically expand reading activity?

10. What information in this chapter will be most helpful to you? Why?

chapter 5: Using Very Small Groups or Tutoring

1. Discuss whether you believe the size of the intervention groups in your district K–2, 3–5, 7–8, or 9–12 are small enough to be effective?

2. What are your thoughts about giving a reading test to pupils with disabilities? Is it a fair assessment of whether or not these pupils are meeting the state reading standards?

3. In your past experiences, do you think that discussions about treatment failures focused on causes lying within the student or causes lying within the treatment? Do you think the focus of such discussions is still the same or changing?

4. In your district how often are struggling readers who are not improving moved from small group instruction to a tutorial lesson design? What factors are used to make the decision?

5. Share with your group ways you have discovered to find time for small group intervention lessons that actually add new minutes of reading instruction for struggling readers.

6. What resources have you already utilized or might investigate as options for funding more small group and tutorial intervention lessons?

7. What is your opinion of Allington's argument that delivering small group intervention services should be part of every district employee's job?

8. After reading this chapter, how will you create more opportunities for struggling readers to receive services in small group or tutoring sessions?

9. What information in this chapter will be most helpful to you? Why?

chapter 6: Coordinating Intervention with Core Classroom

1. Discuss your thoughts on pull-out versus in-class interventions.

2. What are some of the reasons you feel curriculum coordination doesn't always happen (i.e., lack of time to communicate, different philosophies of instruction, belief that special education students learn differently and require different curricula, etc.)?

3. Allington notes four problems associated with defining curriculum coordination. Discuss which of these in your experience you believe contributes most to the lack of coordination.

4. Analyze the reading materials in your classrooms and intervention programs as to whether their text difficulty is determined by the number of high-frequency words, decodable words, or predictability, repetition, and rhyming. Discuss what you discover.

5. Using Allington's definitions of *standard protocol* versus *responsive instruction,* which most closely describes the design of your intervention programs?

6. Allington notes the importance of coordination of reading assessment tools. Identify any reading assessments used in your district, and determine whether this is a coordination issue for you to consider.

7. Identify the philosophical base of intervention instruction versus classroom instruction in your district. Are they similar or is coordination at this level an issue to consider?

8. Discuss whether most of your support for curriculum coordination comes from the federal level, the state level, the district level, or the school level.

9. Allington emphasizes the importance of breadth and balance in intervention designs. Discuss what you feel is their role in developing intervention programs for your students.

10. After reading this chapter, what will you do to coordinate interventions with the core classroom?

11. What information in this chapter will be most helpful to you? Why?

chapter 7:   Delivering Intervention by Expert Teacher

1. Looking at your school's intervention staffing, what percentage of your struggling readers now receive instruction from certified staff? What percentage of those certified staff would you say are expert teachers of reading?

2. Considering what the research says about the effects that paraprofessionals have on student achievement, why do you think the use of paraprofessionals in instructional settings is so prevalent?

3. Allington cites a study by Howes that raises the issue of created dependency when aides worked with lower-achieving students. Discuss whether you think this is true from your experience.

4. In your district have efforts to improve reading achievement focused more often on changing school intervention designs, changing materials, or changing who delivers the instruction?

5. Make a list of any programs/products your school uses for reading instruction and determine what outcomes you are expecting by using them. Check the What Works Clearinghouse information to see if there is research to support using these programs to accomplish your goals. Discuss your findings.

6. Given Allington's belief that good, effective teaching is adaptive teaching, describe how you believe scripted programs and computer programs do or do not provide these adaptations.

7. In your district, do you think teachers receive professional development and support to grow as the effective reading teachers described by Duffy, or is more of their training focused on a certain method or sets of materials?

8. If expert teachers are the kind that Pearson says are wanted and effective interventions require expert teachers, why do you think paraprofessionals, scripted programs, and computer programs are so often part of intervention designs?

9. After reading the chapter, how might you ensure that in your intervention programs, the expert teacher will deliver the instruction?

10. What information in this chapter will be most helpful to you? Why?

chapter 8:   Focusing Instruction on Meta-Cognition and Meaning

1. How much does classroom instruction in your school emphasize decoding? How much does it emphasize meaning? Is this in coordination with the intervention instruction in your school?

2. Do you believe the emphasis of the intervention instruction is determined more by the individual needs of the students, the available programs and materials, or the instructional preferences on the part of the teacher?

3. Discuss whether each of Duke and Pearson's features critical to comprehension development are present in your intervention design.

4. Looking at Keene's traits of exceptional comprehension teachers, which ones do you believe describe your teaching?

5. Why do you think that discussion-based instruction has such an effect on producing higher reading achievement?

6. What have you or others in your school done to minimize the use of worksheets, workbooks, or test preparation materials?

7. Discuss the importance of teachers being expert at good strategy instruction. What are some ways you might suggest to improve this expertise for all teachers?

8. Observe a session where a struggling reader is reading aloud (or videotape yourself in such a session). Note the number and quickness of teacher interruptions, and discuss your findings in reference to what Allington says about "learned helplessness."

9. After reading this chapter, in what ways might you or others in your school focus instruction more on meta-cognition and meaning?

10. What information in this chapter will be most helpful to you? Why?

chapter 9: Using Texts That Are Interesting to Students

1. In addition to Pressley's list of motivating factors found in effective teachers' classrooms, have you found other factors that motivate students?

2. In addition to those on Pressley's list, discuss what other factors you know from your experience that undermine reading motivation.

3. Explain why you believe most interventions do or do not incorporate the factors of Fink's interest-based intervention model.

4. Given the research on the power of student choice, what might you do in your classroom to increase the number of student tasks that allow for choice?

5. Allington offers several suggestions for finding appropriate books for struggling readers. Share with your group other options you have used.

6. Guthrie lists four beliefs he says teachers have. Do you agree or disagree with his argument?

7. Discuss Fillman and Guthrie's list of key teacher behaviors that promote and reduce motivation to read. Do you think there are certain grade levels where you might most often find the motivating teacher behaviors and certain grade levels where you might most often find the unmotivating teacher behaviors? If so, why?

8. Discuss where in your district or school budget you might find money to fund the purchase of more books.

9. After reading this chapter, what might you do to increase the use of texts that are interesting to students?

10. What information in this chapter will be most helpful to you? Why?

chapter 10: Questions and Answers about Interventions

1. In what ways might you use the What Works Clearinghouse list of programs to help improve instruction for students in your district?

2. Given Allington's recommendations for assessment, do you see any changes or refinements you might make for progress monitoring?

3. Considering Allington's comments on computer-based interventions and the lack of research to support their effectiveness, why do you think so many schools use them?

4. Discuss what you think a Reading Recovery type of intervention might look like for struggling readers in the fourth grade.

5. Give your reasons for agreeing or disagreeing with Allington's comments on brain research.

6. Discuss your reaction to Goswami's neuromyths.

7. If you have had experience with a reading coach model, what factors did or did not make it effective?

8. Have you ever taught a student who had been labeled as a dyslexic? What did you learn from that experience?

9. After reading this chapter, were there other questions you might have had Allington answer that were not addressed?

10. What information in this chapter will be most helpful to you? Why?

Reading Reaction Sheet

Facilitator/Recorder (person who initiated the discussion): _____

Group reactants: _____

_____

Date of reaction/discussion: _____

Chapter title and author(s): _____

_____

Question #1: What ideas and information from this chapter could be used in classroom instruction?

Reactions:

Question #2: _____

_____

Reactions:

Question #3: _____

_____

Reactions:

Question #4: _____

_____

Reactions:

Book Study Guide

Bibliography

Achilles, C. M. (1999). *Let's put kids first, finally: Getting class size right.* Thousand Oaks, CA: Corwin Press.

Adams, M. J. (1990). *Beginning to read: Thinking and learning about print.* Cambridge, MA: MIT Press.

Afflerbach, P. (2007). *Understanding and using reading assessment, K–12.* Newark, DE: International Reading Association.

Allington, R. L. (1983). The reading instruction provided readers of differing abilities. *Elementary School Journal, 83,* 548–559.

Allington, R. L. (2002a). *Big brother and the national reading curriculum: How ideology trumped evidence.* Portsmouth, NH: Heinemann.

Allington, R. L. (2002b). Research on reading/learning disability interventions. In A. E. Farstrup & S. J. Samuels (Eds.), *What research says about reading instruction* (3rd ed., pp. 261–290). Newark, DE: International Reading Association.

Allington, R. L. (2002c). What I've learned about effective reading instruction from a decade of studying exemplary elementary classroom teachers. *Phi Delta Kappan, 83*(10), 740–747.

Allington, R. L. (2002d). You can't learn much from books you can't read. *Educational Leadership, 60*(3): 16–19.

Allington, R. L. (2004). Setting the record straight. *Educational Leadership, 61*(6): 22–25.

Allington, R. L. (2006a). Critical factors in designing an effective reading intervention for struggling readers. In C. Cummins (Ed.), *Understanding and implementing Reading First initiatives.* Newark, DE: International Reading Association.

Allington, R. L. (2006b). Research and the Three Tier model. *Reading Today, 23*(5), 20.

Allington, R. L. (2006c). *What really matters for struggling readers: Designing research-based programs* (2nd ed.). Boston, Allyn & Bacon.

Allington, R. L. (2007). Intervention all day long: New hope for struggling readers. *Voices from the Middle, 14*(4), 7–14.

Allington, R. L. (2009). *What really matters in fluency: Research-based practices across the curriculum.* Boston: Allyn & Bacon.

Allington, R. L., & Broikou, K. (1988). The development of shared knowledge: A new role for classroom and specialist teachers. *Reading Teacher, 41*(8), 806–811.

Allington, R. L., Broikou, K., & Jachym, N. (1990). Curriculum coherence through instructional coordination: Improving school programs for at-risk children. *Journal of Educational and Psychological Consultation, 1,* 123–136.

Allington, R. L., & Cunningham, P. M. (2006). *Schools that work: Where all children read and write* (3rd ed.). Boston: Allyn & Bacon.

Allington, R. L., & Johnston, P. (1989). Coordination, collaboration, and consistency: The redesign of compensatory and special education interventions. In R. Slavin, N. Karweit, & N. Malden (Eds.), *Effective programs for students at risk* (pp. 320–354). Boston: Allyn & Bacon.

Allington, R. L., & Johnston, P. (Eds.). (2002). *Reading to learn: Lessons from exemplary 4th grade classrooms.* New York: Guilford.

Allington, R. L., & McGill-Franzen, A. M. (1989). School response to reading failure: Chapter 1 and special education students in grades 2, 4, & 8. *Elementary School Journal, 89*(5), 529–542.

Allington, R. L., & McGill-Franzen, A. M. (2006). Contamination of current accountability systems. *Phi Delta Kappan, 87*(10), 762–766.

Allington, R. L., & McGill-Franzen, A. M. (2008). Comprehension difficulties of struggling readers. In S. Israel & G. G. Duffy (Eds.), *Handbook of comprehension research.* Mahwah, NJ: Lawrence Erlbaum.

Allington, R. L., & Nowak, R. (2004). "Proven programs" and other unscientific ideas. In C. C. Block, D. Lapp, E. J. Cooper, J. Flood, N. Roser, & J. V. Tinajero (Eds.), *Teaching all the children: Strategies for developing literacy in an urban setting* (pp. 93–102). New York: Guilford.

Allington, R. L., & Shake, M. C. (1986). Remedial reading: Achieving curricular congruence in classroom and clinic. *Reading Teacher, 39,* 648–654.

Anders, P. L., Hoffman, J. V., & Duffy, G. G. (2000). Teaching teachers to teach reading: Paradigm shifts, persistent problems, and challenges. In M. Kamil, P. Mosenthal, P. D. Pearson, & R. Barr (Eds.), *Handbook of reading research* (Vol. III, pp. 719–742). Mahwah, NJ: Lawrence Erlbaum.

Anderson, L. W., & Pellicier, L. O. (1990). Synthesis of research on compensatory and remedial education. *Educational Leadership, 48*(1), 10–16.

Applebee, A. N., Langer, J. A., Nystrand, M., & Gamoran, A. (2003). Discussion-based approaches to developing understanding: Classroom instruction and student performance in middle and high school English. *American Educational Research Journal, 40*(3), 685–730.

Applegate, M., Quinn, K., & Applegate, A. (2007). *The critical reading inventory: Assessing students' reading and thinking* (2nd ed.). Pearson Education.

Archambault, M. X. (1989). Instructional setting and other design features of compensatory education programs. In R. E. Slavin, N. Karweit, & N. Madden (Eds.), *Effective programs for students at risk* (pp. 220–263). Boston: Allyn & Bacon.

Bembry, K. L., Jordan, H. R., Gomez, E., Anderson, M., & Mendro, R. L. (1998). *Policy implications of long-term teacher effects on student achievement.* Paper presented at the American Educational Research Association, San Diego, CA.

Bender, W. N., & Shores, C. (2007). *Response to intervention: A practical guide for every teacher.* Thousand Oaks, CA: Corwin.

Berliner, D. C. (1986). In pursuit of the expert pedagogue. *Educational Researcher, 15,* 5–13.

Betts, E. A. (1946). *Foundations of reading instruction.* New York: American Book Co.

Betts, E. A. (1949). Adjusting instruction to individual needs. In N. B. Henry (Ed.), *The forty-eighth yearbook of the national society for the study of education: Part II, Reading in the elementary school* (pp. 266–283). Chicago: University of Chicago Press.

Birman, B. F., Desimone, L., Porter, A. C., & Garet, M. (2000). Designing professional development that works. *Educational Leadership, 57*(8), 28–32.

Borman, G. D., & D'Agostino, J. V. (2001). Title I and student achievement: A quantitative synthesis. In G. D. Borman, S. C. Stringfield, & R. E. Slavin (Eds.), *Title I: Compensatory education at the crossroads* (pp. 25–57). Mahwah, NJ: Lawrence Erlbaum.

Borman, G. D., Wong, K. K., Hedges, L. V., & D'Agostino, J. V. (2003). Coordinating categorical and regular programs: Effects on Title I students' educational opportunities and outcomes. In G. D. Borman, S. C. Stringfield, & R. E. Slavin (Eds.), *Title I: Compensatory education at the crossroads* (pp. 79–116). Mahwah, NJ: Lawrence Erlbaum.

Boyd-Zaharias, J., & Pate-Bain, H. (1998). *Teacher aides and student learning: Lessons from Project Star.* Arlington, VA: Educational Research Service.

Brasseur, I., & Hock, M. (2006). What is the nature of adolescent struggling readers in urban schools? Unpublished paper, University of Kansas.

Brown, K. J., Morris, D., & Fields, M. (2005). Intervention after grade 1: Serving increased number of struggling readers effectively. *Journal of Literacy Research, 37*(1), 61–94.

Brown, R., Pressley, M., Van Meter, P., & Schuder, T. (1996). A quasi-experimental validation of transactional strategies instruction with low-achieving second grade readers. *Journal of Educational Psychology, 88*(1), 18–37.

Buly, M. R., & Valencia, S. W. (2002). Below the bar: Profiles of students who fail state reading assessments. *Educational Evaluation and Policy Analysis, 24*(3), 219–239.

Caldwell, J. S. (2008). *Reading assessment: A primer for teachers and coaches.* New York: Guilford.

Carr, M., Borkowski, J. G., & Maxwell, S. E. (1991). Motivational components of underachievement. *Developmental Psychology, 27*(1), 108–118.

Chall, J. S., & Conard, S. S. (1991). *Should textbooks challenge students?* New York: Teachers College Press.

Clay, M. M. (1985). *The early detection of reading difficulties: A diagnostic survey with recovering procedures* (3rd ed.). Exeter, NH: Heinemann.

Coles, G. (2004). Danger in the classroom: "Brain glitch" research and learning to read. *Phi Delta Kappan, 85*(5), 344–351.

Compton, D. L. (2006). How should "unresponsiveness" to secondary intervention be operationalized? It is all about the nudge. *Journal of Learning Disabilities, 39*(2), 170–173.

Connor, C. M. (2007). Learning environments underlying literacy acquisition. In *Encyclopedia of language and literacy development* (pp. 1–11). London, ON: Canadian Language and Literacy Research Network.

Connor, C. M., Morrison, F. J., Fishman, B. J., Schatschneider, C., & Underwood, P. (2007, January). Algorithm-guided individualized reading instruction. *Science, 315,* 464–465.

Cruickshank, D. R., & Haefele, D. (2001). Good teachers, plural. *Educational Leadership, 58*(5), 26–30.

Cunningham, A. E., Perrya, K. E., Stanovich, K. E., & Share, D. L. (2002). Orthographic learning during reading: Examining the role of self-teaching. *Journal of Experimental Child Psychology, 82*(3), 185–199.

Cunningham, A. E., & Stanovich, K. E. (1998). The impact of print exposure on word recognition. In J. Metsala & L. Ehri (Eds.), *Word recognition in beginning literacy* (pp. 235–262). Mahwah, NJ: Lawrence Erlbaum.

Cunningham, P. M., & Allington, R. L. (2007). *Classrooms that work: They can all read and write* (4th ed.). Boston: Allyn & Bacon.

Cushman, K. (2003). *Fires in the bathroom: Advice for teachers from high school students.* New York: The New Press.

D'Agostino, J. V., & Murphy, J. A. (2004). A meta-analysis of Reading Recovery in United States schools. *Educational Evaluation and Policy Analysis, 26*(1), 23–38.

Dahl, K. L., & Freppon, P. A. (1995). A comparison of inner-city children's interpretations of reading and writing instruction in skills-based and whole language classrooms. *Reading Research Quarterly, 30,* 50–74.

Denton, C. A., Vaughn, S., & Fletcher, J. M. (2003). Bringing research-based practice in reading intervention to scale. *Learning Disabilities Research and Practice, 18*(3), 201–211.

Dolch, E. W. (1936). A basic sight vocabulary. *Elementary School Journal, 36,* 456–460.

Duffy, G. G. (1993). Teachers' progress toward becoming expert strategy teachers. *Elementary School Journal, 94*(2), 109–120.

Duffy, G. G. (2003). *Explaining reading: A resource for teaching concepts, skills, and strategies.* New York: Guilford.

Duffy, G. G. (2004). Teachers who improve reading achievement: What research says about what they do and how to develop them. In D. Strickland & M. Kamil (Eds.), *Improving reading achievement through professional development* (pp. 3–22). Norwood, MA: Christopher-Gordon.

Duke, N. K. (2000). 3.6 minutes per day: The scarcity of informational texts in first grade. *Reading Research Quarterly, 35*(2), 202–224.

Duke, N. K., & Bennett-Armistead, S. (2003). *Reading and writing informational text in the primary grades.* New York: Scholastic.

Duke, N. K., & Pearson, P. D. (2002). Effective practices for developing reading comprehension. In A. E. Farstrup & S. J. Samuels (Eds.), *What research says about reading instruction* (3rd ed., pp. 205–242). Newark, DE: International Reading Association.

Duke, N. K., Pressley, M., & Hilden, K. (2004). Difficulties with reading comprehension. In C. A. Stone, E. R. Silliman, B. J. Ehren, & K. Apel (Eds.), *Handbook of language and literacy: Development and disorders* (pp. 501–520). New York: Guilford.

Ehri, L. C., Dreyer, L. G., Flugman, B., & Gross, A. (2007). Reading Rescue: An effective tutoring intervention model for language minority students who are struggling readers in first grade. *American Educational Research Journal, 44*(2), 414–448.

Elbaum, B., Vaughn, S., Hughes, M. J., & Moody, S. W. (2000). How effective are one-to-one tutoring programs in reading for elementary students at risk for reading failure? A meta-analysis of the intervention research. *Journal of Educational Psychology, 92*(4), 605–619.

Fillman, S., & Guthrie, J. T. (2008). Control and choice: Supporting self-directed reading. In J. T. Guthrie (Ed.), *Engaging adolescents in reading* (pp. 33–48). Thousand Oaks, CA: Corwin.

Fink, R. (1998). Literacy in successful men and women with dyslexia. *Annals of Dyslexia, 48,* 311–346.

Fink, R. (2006). *Why Jane and Johnny couldn't read— and how they learned.* Newark, DE: International Reading Association.

Fink, R., & Samuels, S. J. (2008). *Inspiring reading success: Interest and motivation in an age of high-stakes testing.* Newark, DE: International Reading Association.

Finn, J. D., & Achilles, C. M. (1990). Answers and questions about class size: A statewide experiment. *American Educational Research Journal, 27*(3), 557–577.

Fisher, C. W., & Berliner, D. C. (1985). *Perspectives on instructional time.* New York: Longmans.

Foorman, B. R., Chen, D., Carlson, C., Moats, L., Francis, D. J., & Fletcher, J. M. (2003). The necessity of the alphabetic principle to phonemic awareness instruction. *Reading and Writing: An Interdisciplinary Journal, 16,* 289–324.

Foorman, B. R., Francis, D. J., Fletcher, J. M., & Schatschneider, C. (1998). The role of instruction in learning to read: Preventing reading failure in at-risk children. *Journal of Educational Psychology, 90*(1), 37–55.

Foorman, B. R., & Moats, L. C. (2004). Conditions for sustaining research-based practices in early reading instruction. *Remedial and Special Education, 25*(1), 51–60.

Foorman, B. R., & Torgeson, J. (2001). Critical elements of classroom and small-group instruction promote reading success in all children. *Learning Disabilities Research and Practice, 16*(4), 203–212.

Fuchs, D., & Fuchs, L. S. (2005). Responsiveness to intervention: A blueprint for practitioners, policy makers and parents. *Teaching Exceptional Children, 38*(1), 57–61.

Fuchs, D., & Fuchs, L. S. (2006). Introduction to response to intervention: What, why, and how valid is it? *Reading Research Quarterly, 41*(1), 93–99.

Fuchs, D., Fuchs, L. S., Thompson, A., Al Otaiba, S., Yen, L., Yang, N., et al. (2001). Is reading important in a reading-readiness program? A randomised field trial with teachers as program implementers. *Journal of Educational Psychology, 93*(2), 251–267.

Fuchs, D., Mock, D., Morgan, P. L., & Young, C. L. (2003). Responsiveness-to-intervention: Definitions, evidence, and implications for the learning disabilities construct. *Learning Disabilities: Theory and Practice, 18*(3), 157–171.

Gambrell, L. B. (1996). Creating classroom cultures that foster motivation to read. *Reading Teacher, 50*(1), 4–25.

Gaskins, I. W. (2008). Ten tenets of motivation for teaching struggling readers—and the rest of the class. In R. Fink & S. J. Samuels (Eds.), *Inspiring reading success: Interest and motivation in an age of high-stakes testing* (pp. 98–116). Newark, DE: International Reading Association.

Gaskins, I. W., Ehri, L. C., Cress, C., O'Hara, C., & Donnelly, K. (1997). Procedures for word learning: Making discoveries about words. *Reading Teacher, 50*(4), 312–327.

Gelzheiser, L. M. (2005). Maximizing student progress in one-to-one programs: Contributions of texts, volunteer experience, and student characteristics. *Exceptionality, 13*(4), 229–243.

Gerber, S. B., Finn, J. D., Achilles, C. M., & Boyd-Zaharias, J. (2001). Teacher aides and students' academic achievement. *Educational Evaluation and Policy Analysis, 23*(2), 123–143.

German, D., & Newman, J. R. S. (2007). Oral reading skills of children with oral language (word-finding) difficulties. *Reading Psychology, 28*(5), 397–442.

Gersten, R., Fuchs, L. S., Williams, J. P., & Baker, S. (2001). Teaching reading comprehension strategies to students with learning disabilities: A review of the research. *Review of Educational Research, 71*(2), 279–320.

Goswami, U. (2004). Neuroscience, education, and special education. *British Journal of Special Education, 31*(4), 175–183.

Gray, C., McCoy, S., Dunbar, C., Dunn, J., Mitchell, D., & Ferguson, J. (2007). Added value or a familiar face: The impact of learning assistants on young readers. *Journal of Early Childhood Research, 5*(3), 285–300.

Guice, S., Allington, R. L., Johnston, P., Baker, K., & Michelson, N. (1996). Access? Books, children, and literature-based curriculum in schools. *The New Advocate, 9*(3), 197–207.

Guthrie, J. T. (2004). Teaching for literacy engagement. *Journal of Literacy Research, 36*(1), 1–28.

Guthrie, J. T. (2008). Growing motivation: How students develop. In J. T. Guthrie (Ed.), *Engaging adolescents in reading* (pp. 99–113). Thousand Oaks, CA: Corwin Press.

Guthrie, J. T., & Humenick, N. M. (2004). Motivating students to read: Evidence for classroom practices that increase motivation and achievement. In P. McCardle & V. Chhabra (Eds.), *The voice of evidence in reading research.* Baltimore: Paul Brookes.

Guthrie, J. T., Wigfield, A., Metsala, J. L., & Cox, K. E. (1999). Motivational and cognitive predictors of text comprehension and reading amount. *Scientific Studies of Reading, 3*(3), 231–256.

Hammill, D. D. (2004). What we know about correlates of reading. *Exceptional Children, 70*(4), 453–468.

Hart, B. M., & Risley, T. R. (1995). *Meaningful differences in the everyday experiences of young children.* Baltimore, MD: Paul Brookes.

Hidi, S., & Harackiewicz, J. M. (2000). Motivating the academically unmotivated: A critical issue for the 21st century. *Review of Educational Research, 70*(2), 151–179.

Hiebert, E. H. (1983). An examination of ability grouping for reading instruction. *Reading Research Quarterly, 18*, 231–255.

Hiebert, E. H. (1999). Text matters in learning to read. *Reading Teacher, 52*(6), 552–556.

Hiebert, E. H. (2002). Standards, assessments, and text difficulty. In A. Farstrup & S. J. Samuels (Eds.), *What research has to say about reading instruction* (pp. 337–369). Newark, DE: International Reading Association.

Hiebert, E. H., Colt, J. M., Catto, S. L., & Gury, E. C. (1992). Reading and writing of first-grade students in a restructured Chapter 1 program. *American Educational Research Journal, 29*(3), 545–572.

Hiebert, E. H., & Fisher, C. W. (2006). Fluency from the first: What works with first graders. In T. Rasinski, C. Blachowicz & K. Lems (Eds.), *Fluency instruction: Research-based best practices* (pp. 279–295). New York: Guilford.

Hiebert, E. H., & Taylor, B. M. (2000). Beginning reading instruction: Research on early intervention. In M. Kamil, P. Mosenthal, P. D. Pearson, & R. Barr (Eds.), *Handbook of reading research* (Vol. III, pp. 455–482). Mahwah, NJ: Lawrence Erlbaum.

Hoffman, J. V., Roller, C. M., Maloch, B., Sailors, M., & Beretvas, N. (2003). *Prepared to make a difference: Final report of the national commission on excellence in elementary teacher preparation for reading.* Newark, DE: International Reading Association.

Howes, A. (2003). Teaching reforms and the impact of paid adult support on participation and learning in mainstream schools. *Support for learning, 18*(4), 147–153.

Individuals with Disabilities Education Act. (2004). P. L. 108–446, Sec. 614, 118 Stat. Retrieved on November 22, 2007, from www.copaa.org/pdf/IDEA2004.pdf.

International Reading Association, (1994, Spring). Who is teaching our children? Implications of the use of aides in Chapter 1. *ERS Spectrum,* 28–34.

Invernezzi, M. A. (2001). The complex world of one-on-one tutoring. In S. Neuman & D. Dickinson (Eds.), *Handbook of early literacy research* (pp. 459–470). New York: Guilford.

Jachym, N., Allington, R. L., & Broikou, K. A. (1989). Estimating the cost of seatwork. *Reading Teacher, 43*(1), 30–37.

Jenkins, J. R., Pious, C., & Peterson, D. (1988). Categorical programs for remedial and handicapped students: Issues of validity. *Exceptional Children, 55*(2), 147–158.

Johnston, P. (2000). *Running records: A self-tutoring guide.* Portland, ME: Stenhouse.

Johnston, P. (2005). *Choice words.* Portland, ME: Stenhouse.

Johnston, P., & Allington, R. L. (1990). Remediation. In P. D. Pearson (Ed.), *Handbook of reading research* (Vol. III, pp. 984–1012). New York: Longmans.

Johnston, P., Allington, R. L., & Afflerbach, P. (1985). The congruence of classroom and remedial reading instruction. *Elementary School Journal, 85,* 465–478.

Johnston, P., & Winograd, (1985). Passive failure in reading. *Journal of Reading Behavior, 17,* 279–301.

Keene, E. O. (2002). From good to memorable: Characteristics of highly effective comprehension teaching. In C. C. Block, L. Gambrell, & M. Pressley (Eds.), *Improving comprehension instruction: Rethinking research, theory, and classroom practice* (pp. 80–105). San Francisco: Jossey-Bass.

Keene, E. O. (2008). *To understand: New horizons in reading comprehension.* Portsmouth, NH: Heinemann.

Keene, E. O., & Zimmerman, S. (2007). *Mosaic of thought: Teaching comprehension in a reader's workshop.* Portsmouth, NH: Heinemann.

Knapp, M. S. (1995). *Teaching for meaning in high-poverty classrooms.* New York: Teachers College Press.

Knapp, M. S., & Shields, P. M. (Eds.). (1991). *Better schooling for the children of poverty: Alternatives to conventional wisdom.* Berkeley, CA: McCutchan.

Knapp, M. S., Shields, P. M., & Turnbull, B. J. (1992). *Academic challenge for the children of poverty: Summary report.* Washington, DC: U.S. Department of Education, Office of Policy and Planning.

Kuhn, M. R. (2005). A comparative study of small group fluency instruction. *Reading Psychology, 26*(2), 127–146.

Kuhn, M. R., Schwanenflugel, P., Morris, R. D., Morrow, L. M., Woo, D., Meisinger, B., et al. (2006). Teaching children to become fluent and automatic readers. *Journal of Literacy Research, 38*(4), 357–388.

Kuhn, M. R., & Stahl, S. A. (2003). Fluency: A review of developmental and remedial practices. *Journal of Educational Psychology, 95*(1), 3–21.

Langer, J. A. (2001). Beating the odds: Teaching middle and high school students to read and write well. *American Educational Research Journal, 38*(4), 837–880.

Leach, J. M., Scarborough, H. S., & Rescorda, L. (2003). Late-emerging reading disabilities. *Journal of Educational Psychology, 95*(2), 211–224.

Leinhardt, G., Zigmond, N., & Cooley, W. (1981). Reading instruction and its effects. *American Educational Research Journal, 18*(3), 343–361.

Leslie, L., & Caldwell, J. S. (2006). *Qualitative reading inventory 4.* Boston: Allyn & Bacon.

Lewis, M., & Samuels, S. J. (2004). *Read more, read better? A meta-analysis of the literature on the relationship between exposure to reading and reading achievement.* Unpublished paper. Minneapolis: University of Minnesota.

Lose, M. K. (2007). A child's response to intervention requires a responsive teacher of reading. *Reading Teacher, 61*(3), 276–279.

Lyon, G. R., Fletcher, J. M., Shaywitz, S. E., Shaywitz, B. A, Torgeson, J. K., Wood, F. B., Schulte, A. & Olson, R. (2001). Rethinking learning disabilities. In C. E. Finn, R. A. J. Rotherham, & C. R. Hokanson (Eds.), *Rethinking special education for a new century* (pp. 259–287). Washington, DC: Progressive Policy Institute and the Thomas B. Fordham Foundation.

Lyons, C. A., & Beaver, J. (2007). Reducing retention and learning disability placement through Reading Recovery: An educationally sound, cost-effective choice. In R. L. Allington & S. A. Walmsley (Eds.), *No quick fix: The RTI edition* (pp. 116–136). New York: Teachers College Press.

Mastropieri, M. A., & Scruggs, T. E. (1997). Best practices in promoting reading comprehension in students with learning disabilities, 1976–1996. *Remedial and Special Education, 18*(4), 197–213.

Mastropieri, M. A., Scruggs, T. E., Bakken, J. P., & Whedon, C. (1996). Reading comprehension: A synthesis of research in learning disabilities. In T. E. Scruggs & M. A. Mastropieri (Eds.), *Advances in learning and behavioral disabilities* (Vol. 10, part B, pp. 201–227). Greenwich, CT: JAI Press.

Mathes, P. G., Denton, C. A., Fletcher, J. M., Anthony, J. L., Francis, D. J. & Schatschneider, C. (2005). The effects of theoretically different instruction and student characteristics on the skills of struggling readers. *Reading Research Quarterly, 40*(2): 148–182.

Mathson, D. (2006, December). *Co-constructing the implementation of multi-level texts in middle school science classrooms.* Paper presented at the National Reading Conference, Los Angeles.

McEneaney, J. E., Lose, M. K., & Schwartz, R. M. (2006). A transactional perspective on reading difficulties and response to intervention. *Reading Research Quarterly, 41*(1), 117–128.

McGill-Franzen, A. M. (1993). "I could read the words!" Selecting good books for inexperienced readers. *Reading Teacher, 46*(6), 424–426.

McGill-Franzen, A. M. (2006). *Kindergarten literacy.* New York: Scholastic.

McGill-Franzen, A. M., & Allington, R. L. (1990). Comprehension and coherence: Neglected elements of literacy instruction in remedial and resource room services. *Journal of Reading, Writing, and Learning Disabilities, 6*(2), 149–182.

McGill-Franzen, A. M., & Allington, R. L. (2006). Contamination of current accountability systems. *Phi Delta Kappan, 87*(10), 762–766.

McGill-Franzen, A. M., & Allington, R. L. (2008). Got books? *Educational Leadership, 65*(7), 20–23.

McGill-Franzen, A. M., Allington, R. L., Yokoi, L., & Brooks, G. (1999). Putting books in the classroom seems necessary but not sufficient. *Journal of Educational Research, 93*(2), 67–74.

McGill-Franzen, A. M., Zmach, C., Solic, K., & Zeig, J. L. (2006). The confluence of two policy mandates: Core reading programs and third-grade retention in Florida. *Elementary School Journal, 107*(1), 67–91.

McIntyre, E., & Freppon, P. A. (1994). A comparison of children's development of alphabetic knowledge in a skills-based and a whole language classroom. *Research in the Teaching of English, 28*(4), 391–417.

McIntyre, E., Rightmeyer, E., Powell, R., Powers, S., & Petrosko, J. (2006). How much should young children read? A study of the relationship between development and instruction. *Literacy Teaching and Learning, 11*(1), 51–72.

McQuillan, J. (1997). The effects of incentives on reading. *Reading Research and Instruction, 36*(2), 111–125.

Mellard, D. F., & Johnson, E. (2008). *RTI: A practitioner's guide to implementing response to intervention.* Thousand Oaks, CA: Corwin Press.

Mercer, C. D. & Mercer, A. R. (2001). *Teaching students with learning problems* (5th ed.). Columbus, OH: Merrill/Prentice-Hall.

Mesmer, H. A. E. (2008). *Tools for matching readers to texts: Research-based practices.* New York: Guilford.

Nation, K. (2005). Children's reading comprehension difficulties. In M. Snowling & C. Hulme (Eds.), *The science of reading: A handbook* (pp. 248–265). Oxford, U.K.: Blackwell.

National Center for Educational Statistics. (1995). *Listening to children read aloud: Oral fluency* (No. NCES 95–762r). Washington, DC: U.S. Department of Education.

National Center for Educational Statistics. (2004). *Who teaches reading in public elementary schools? The assignments and educational preparation of reading teachers* (Issue Brief No. NCES2004–034). Washington, DC: U.S. Department of Education, Institute of Education Sciences.

New York State Reading Association takes active role in RTI professional development. (2007, October/November). *Reading Today,* pp. 10–11.

Norwich, B., & Lewis, A. (2007). How specialized is teaching children with disabilities and difficulties? *Journal of Curriculum Studies, 39*(2), 127–150

Nye, B., Konstantopoulos, S., & Hedges, L. V. (2004). How large are teacher effects? *Educational Evaluation and Policy Analysis, 26*(3), 237–257.

O'Connor, E. A., & Simic, O. (2002). The effect of Reading Recovery on special education referrals and placements. *Psychology in the Schools, 39*, 635–646.

O'Connor, R. E., Bell, K. M., Harty, K. R., Larkin, L. K., Sackor, S.M, & Zigmond N. (2002). Teaching reading to poor readers in the intermediate grades: A comparison of text difficulty. *Journal of Educational Psychology, 94*(3): 474–485.

O'Connor, R. E., & Harty, K. (2005, April 12). *Response to treatment as an early indicator of reading disability.* Paper presented at the American Educational Research Association, Montreal.

Pearson, P. D. (2003). The role of professional knowledge in reading reform. *Language Arts, 81*(1), 14–15.

Phillips, L. M., Norris, S. P., & Steffler, D. J. (2007). Potential risks to reading posed by high-dose phonics. *Journal of Applied Research on Learning, 1*(1), 1–18.

Pickett, A. L. (1996). *A state of the art report on paraeducators in education and related services.* New York: National Resource Center for Paraprofessionals in Education and Related Services, Center for Advanced Study in Education, The Graduate School & University Center, City University of New York.

Pinnell, G. S., Lyons, C. A., DeFord, D. E., Bryk, A. S., & Seltzer, M. (1994). Comparing instructional models for the literacy education of high-risk first graders. *Reading Research Quarterly, 29*(1), 8–39.

Pinnell, G. S., Pikulski, J. J., Wixson, K., Campbell, J. R., Gough, P. B., & Beatty, A. S. (1995). *Listening to children read aloud.* (Research report No. ED 378550). Washington, DC: National Center for Educational Statistics.

Pokorni, J. L., Worthington, C. K., & Jamison, P. J. (2004). Phonological awareness intervention: Comparison of Fast ForWord, Earobics, and LIPS. *Journal of Educational Research, 97*(3), 147–157.

Pressley, M. (2002). Effective beginning reading instruction. *Journal of Literacy Research, 34*(2), 165–188.

Pressley, M. (2006) *Reading instruction that really works* (3rd ed.). New York: Guilford.

Pressley, M., Allington, R. L., Wharton-MacDonald, R., Collins-Block, C., & Morrow, L. (2001). *Learning to read: Lessons from exemplary first-grade classrooms.* New York: Guilford.

Pressley, M., Dolezal, S. E., Raphael, L. M., Mohan, L., Roehrig, A. D., & Bogner, K. (2003). *Motivating primary grade students.* New York: Guilford.

Puma, M. J., Karweit, N., Price, C., Ricciuti, A., Thompson, W., & Vaden-Kiernan, M. (1997). *Prospects: Final report on student outcomes.* Washington, DC: U.S. Department of Education, Office of Planning and Evaluation Services.

Rasinski, T. V., & Hoffman, J. V. (2003). Oral reading in the school literacy curriculum. *Reading Research Quarterly, 38*(4), 510–523.

Rayner, K., Foorman, B. R., Perfetti, C. A., Pesetsky, D., & Seidenberg, M. S. (2002). How psychological science informs the teaching of reading. *Psychological Science in the Public Interest, 2*(2), 31–74.

Reis, S. M., McCoach, D. B., Coyne, M., Schreiber, F. J., Eckert, R. D., & Gubbins, E. J. (2007). Using planned enrichment strategies with direct instruction to improve reading fluency, comprehension, and attitude toward reading: An evidence-based study. *Elementary School Journal, 108*(1), 3–24.

Ross, J. A. (2004). Effects of running records assessment on early literacy achievement. *Journal of Educational Research, 97*(2), 186–195.

Roth, J., Brooks-Dunn, J., Linver, M., & Hofferth, S. (2002). What happened during the school day? Time diaries from a national sample of elementary school teachers. *Teachers College Record, 105*(3), 317–343.

Rouse, C. E., & Krueger, A. B. (2004). Putting computerized instruction to the test: A randomized evaluation of a "scientifically-based" reading program. *Economics of Education Review, 23*(4), 323–338.

Rowan, B., & Guthrie, L. F. (1989). The quality of Chapter I instruction: Results from a study of twenty-four schools. In R. E. Slavin, N. Karweit, & N. Madden (Eds.), *Effective programs for students at risk* (pp. 195–219). Boston: Allyn & Bacon.

Rowan, B., Guthrie, L. F., Lee, G. V., & Guthrie, G. P. (1986). *The design and implementation of Chapter 1 instructional services: A study of 24 schools.* San Francisco: Far West Laboratory for Educational Research and Development.

Rupp, A. A., & Lesaux, N. K. (2006). Meeting expectations? An empirical investigation of a standards-based assessment of reading comprehension. *Educational Evaluation and Policy Analysis, 28*(4), 315–333.

Samuels, S. J. (2007). The DIBELS tests: Is speed of barking at print what we mean by reading fluency? *Reading Research Quarterly, 42*(4), 563–566.

Samuels, S. J., & Wu, Y. C. (2003). *How the amount of time spent on reading effects reading achievement: A response to the National Reading Panel.* Minneapolis: University of Minnesota.

Sanders, W. L. (1998, December). Value-added assessment. *School Administrator, 55,* 101–113.

Scanlon, D. M., Vellutino, F. R., Small, S. G, Fanuele, D. P., & Sweeney, J. M. (2005). Severe reading difficulties—can they be prevented? A comparison of prevention and intervention approaches. *Exceptionality, 13*(4), 209–227.

Schmidt, R. (2008). Really reading: What does Accelerated Reader teach adults and children? *Language Arts, 85*(3).

Schraw, G., Flowerday, T., & Reisletter, M. F. (1998). The role of choice in reader engagement. *Journal of Educational Psychology, 90,* 705–714.

Schwartz, R. M. (2005). Literacy learning of at-risk first-grade students in the Reading Recovery early intervention. *Journal of Educational Psychology, 97*(2), 257–267.

Shanahan, T. (1998). On the effectiveness and limitations of tutoring. In P. D. Pearson & P. A. Iran-Nejad (Ed.), *Review of research in education* (Vol. 23, pp. 217–234). Washington, DC: American Educational Research Association.

Shanahan, T. (1999). Qualified teachers mean quality reading for needy kids. *Michigan Reading Journal, 31*(3), 5–7.

Shanahan, T. (2002, May 22). Reading report's unending debate. *Education Week,* p. 38.

Share, D. L. (1995). Phonological recoding and self-teaching: Sine qua non of reading acquisition. *Cognition, 55,* 151–218.

Shaywitz, S. E. (1996, November). Dyslexia. *Scientific American,* 98–104.

Shaywitz, S. E., Escobar, M., Shaywitz, M., Fletcher, J., & Makuch, R. (1992). Evidence that dyslexia may represent the lower tail of a normal distribution of reading ability. *New England Journal of Medicine, 326,* 145–150.

Shin, F. H. & Krashen, S. D. (2008). *Summer reading: Program and evidence.* Boston: Allyn & Bacon.

Shinn, M. R. (1989). *Curriculum-based assessment: Assessing special children.* New York: Guilford.

Showers, B., Joyce, B., Scanlon, M., & Schnaubelt, C. (1998, March). A second chance to learn to read. *Educational Leadership, 72,* 27–30.

Slavin, R. E. (2007). The What Works Clearinghouse: Time for a fresh start. *Education Week, 27,* 31.

Snow, C. E., Burns, M. S., & Griffin, P. (1998). *Preventing reading difficulties in young children: A report of the National Research Council.* Washington, DC: National Academy Press.

Stahl, S. A. (2003). No more "madfaces": Motivation and fluency development with struggling readers. In D. M. Barone & L. M. Morrow (Eds.), *Literacy and young children* (pp. 195–209). New York: Guilford.

Stahl, S. A., & Heubach, K. (2005). Fluency oriented reading instruction. *Journal of Literacy Research, 37*(1), 25–60.

Stanovich, K. E., West, R. F., Cunningham, A. E., Cipielewski, J., & Siddiqui, S. (1996). The role of inadequate print exposure as a determinate of reading comprehension problems. In C. Cornoldi & J. Oakhill (Eds.), *Reading comprehension difficulties: Processes and intervention* (pp. 15–32). Mahwah, NJ: Lawrence Erlbaum.

Swanson, H., & Hoskyn, M. (1998). Experimental intervention research on students with learning disabilities: A meta-analysis of treatment outcomes. *Review of Educational Research, 68*(3), 277–321.

Swanson, H., Hoskyn, M., & Lee, C. (1999). *Interventions for students with learning disabilities.* New York: Guilford.

Taylor, B., Short, R., Shearer, B., & Frye, B. (2007). First grade teachers provide early reading intervention in the classroom. In R. L. Allington & S. A. Walmsley (Eds.), *No quick fix: Redesigning literacy programs in America's elementary schools, The RTI edition* (pp. 159–178). New York: Teachers College Press.

Taylor, B. M., Pearson, P. D., Clark, K., & Walpole, S. (2000). Effective Schools and accomplished teachers: Lessons about primary grade reading instruction in low-income schools. *Elementary School Journal 101,* 121–165.

Taylor, B. M., Pearson, P. D., Peterson, D. S., & Rodriguez, M. C. (2003). Reading growth in high-poverty classrooms: The influences of teacher practices that encourage cognitive engagement in literacy learning. *Elementary School Journal, 104*(1), 4–28.

Thurlow, M. L., Ysseldyke, J. E., Graden, J. L., & Algozzine, B. (1983). What's "special" about the special education resource room for learning disabled students? *Learning Disability Quarterly, 6,* 283–288.

Thurlow, M. L., Ysseldyke, J. E., Wotruba, J. W., & Algozzine, B. (1993). Instruction in special education classrooms under varying student-teacher ratios. *Elementary School Journal, 93*(3), 304–320.

Torgeson, J. K. (2000). Individual differences in response to early interventions in reading: The lingering problem of treatment resisters. *Learning Disabilities Research and Practice, 15*(1), 55–64.

Torgeson, J. K. (2002a). Lessons learned from intervention research in reading: A way to go before we rest. *Learning and Teaching Reading,* pp. 89–103.

Torgeson, J. K. (2002b). The prevention of reading difficulties. *Journal of School Psychology, 40*(1), 7–26.

Torgeson, J. K., Alexander, A. W., Wagner, R. K., Rashotte, C. A., Voeller, K. K., Conway, T., et al. (2001). Intensive remedial instruction for children with severe reading disabilities: Immediate and long-term outcomes from two instructional approaches. *Journal of Learning Disabilities, 34*(1), 33–58.

Torgeson, J. K., & Hudson, R. F. (2006). Reading fluency: Critical issues for struggling readers. In S. J. Samuels & A. E. Farstrup (Eds.), *What research has to say about fluency instruction* (pp. 130–158). Newark, DE: International Reading Association.

Torgeson, J. K., Wagner, R. K., & Rashotte, C. A. (1997). Prevention and remediation of severe reading disabilities: Keeping the end in mind. *Scientific Studies of Reading, 1*(3), 217–234.

Turner, J. C. (1995). The influence of classroom contexts on young children's motivation for literacy. *Reading Research Quarterly, 30*(3), 410–441.

U.S. Department of Education. (2005). *Identifying and implementing educational practices supported by rigorous evidence: A user friendly guide,* Washington, DC: U.S. Department of Education.

U.S. Department of Education. (2000). *Study of education resources and federal funding: Final report.* Washington, DC: Planning and Evaluation Service.

Vaughn, S., Gersten, R., & Chard, D. J. (2000). The underlying message in LD intervention research: Findings from research syntheses. *Exceptional Children, 67*(1), 99–114.

Vaughn, S., Linan-Thompson, S., Kouzekanani, K., Bryant, D. P., Dickson, S., & Blozis, S. A. (2003). Reading instruction grouping for students with reading difficulties. *Remedial and Special Education, 24*(5), 301–315.

Vaughn, S., Moody, S. W., & Schumm, J. S. (1998). Broken promises: Reading instruction in the resource room. *Exceptional Children, 64,* 211–225.

Vaughn, S., Wanzek, J., & Fletcher, J. M. (2007). Multiple tiers of intervention: A framework for prevention and identification of students with reading/learning disabilities. In B. M. Taylor & J. E. Ysseldyke (Eds.), *Effective intervention for struggling readers, K–6* (pp. 173–195). New York: Teachers College Press.

Vellutino, F. R. (2003). Individual differences as sources of variability in reading comprehension in elementary school children. In A. P. Sweet & C. E. Snow (Eds.), *Rethinking reading comprehension* (pp. 51–81). New York: Guilford.

Vellutino, F. R., & Fletcher, J. M. (2005). Developmental dyslexia. In M. S. C. Hulme (Ed.), *The science of reading: A handbook* (pp. 362–378). Malden, MA: Blackwell.

Vellutino, F. R., Fletcher, J. M., Snowling, M. J., & Scanlon, D. M. (2004). Specific reading disability (dyslexia): What learned in the past four decades? *Journal of Child Psychology and Psychiatry, 45*(1), 2–40.

Vellutino, F. R., Scanlon, D. M., Small, S., & Fanuele, D. P. (2006). Response to intervention as a vehicle for distinguishing between children with and without reading disabilities: Evidence for the role of kindergarten and first-grade interventions. *Journal of Learning Disabilities, 39*(2), 157–169.

Vellutino, F. R., Sipay, E. R., Small, S. G., Pratt, A., Chen, R., & Denckla, M. B. (1996). Cognitive profiles of difficult-to-remediate and readily remediated poor readers: Early intervention as a vehicle for distinguishing between cognitive and experiential deficits as basic causes of specific reading disability. *Journal of Educational Psychology, 88*(4), 601–638.

Viadero, D. (1992, August 15). Report finds record jump in special education enrollment. *Education Week,* pp. 11, 19.

Walczyk, J. A., & Griffith-Ross, D. A. (2007). How important is reading skill fluency for comprehension? *Reading Teacher, 60*(6), 560–569.

Walker, B. J. (2004). *Diagnostic teaching of reading* (3rd ed.). Upper Saddle River, NJ: Pearson Education.

Walmsley, S. A., & Allington, R. L. (1995). Redefining and reforming instructional support programs for at-risk students. In R. L. Allington & S. A. Walmsley (Eds.), *No quick fix: Rethinking literacy programs in America's elementary schools* (pp. 19–41). New York: Teachers College Press.

Walp, T. P., & Walmsley, S. A. (2007). Scoring well on tests or becoming genuinely literate: Rethinking remediation in a small rural school. In R. L. Allington & S. A. Walmsley (Eds.), *No quick fix: Rethinking literacy programs in America's elementary schools, The RTI edition* (pp. 177–196). New York: Teachers College Press.

Wasik, B. A. (1998). Using volunteers as reading tutors: Guidelines for successful practices. *Reading Teacher, 51,* 562–570.

Wasik, B. A., & Slavin, R. E. (1993). Preventing early reading failure with one-to-one tutoring: A review of five programs. *Reading Research Quarterly, 28*(2), 178–200.

What Works Clearinghouse. (2007). *Effectiveness ratings for beginning reading programs in four domains.* Retrieved on February 15, 2008, from www.whatworks.ed.gov.

White, T. G., Graves, M. F., & Slater, W. H. (1990). Growth of reading vocabulary in diverse elementary schools: Decoding and word meaning. *Journal of Educational Psychology, 82*(2), 281–290.

Williams, J. P. (2002). Reading comprehension strategies and teacher preparation. In A. Farstrup & S. J. Samuels (Eds.), *What research has to say about reading instruction* (pp. 243–260). Newark, DE: International Reading Association.

Xue, Y., & Meisels, S. J. (2004). Early literacy instruction and learning in kindergarten: Evidence from the early childhood longitudinal study—Kindergarten class of 1998–1999. *American Educational Research Journal, 41*(1), 191–229.

Ysseldyke, J. E., O'Sullivan, P. J., Thurlow, M. L., & Christenson, S. L. (1989). Qualitative differences in reading and math instruction received by handicapped students. *Remedial and Special Education, 10*(1), 14–20.

Ysseldyke, J. E., Thurlow, M. L., Mecklenburg, C., & Graden, J. (1984). Opportunity to learn for regular and special education students during reading instruction. *Remedial and Special Education, 5*(1), 29–37.

Zigmond, N., Vallecorsa, A., & Leinhardt, G. (1980). Reading instruction for students with learning disabilities. *Topics in Language Disorders, 1,* 89–98.

Zirkel, P. A. (2006). *SLD eligibility: A users' guide to the new regulations.* Lawrence, KS: National Research Center on Learning Disabilities.

Index